POLITICS and SOCIETY
in MEXICO

POLITICS
and SOCIETY
in MEXICO

BY MARTIN C. NEEDLER

Albuquerque
UNIVERSITY OF NEW MEXICO PRESS

JL
1231
N44

TO EMILIO PORTES GIL
WHO ALWAYS TRIED TO KEEP THE FAITH

PREFACE

In the fall of 1957 the author of this book was a graduate student in political science at Harvard looking for a topic on which to write his doctoral dissertation. At the time he was best acquainted with politics in England, where he had been born and raised, and in Germany, where he had done his military service. He had moreover long been interested in the problem of the rise of Hitler, which at the time called for systematic study (this was before the arrival in Cambridge of Bracher's *Die Auflösung der Weimarer Republik*). But he was also curious about Latin American politics, in those pre-Fidel days a neglected area and one not taught at Harvard, which seemed to him to offer an unequalled wealth of political experience still to be tapped.

Two articles in the *American Political Science Review* indicated the direction in which a solution might be found, Leon Vincent Padgett's "Mexico's One-Party System: a Re-evaluation"[1] and a discussion of the unpublished version of what later became Anthony Downs's *An Economic Theory of Democracy*.[2] Downs's work suggested the predictive power of models of rational action deduced from the formal characteristics of competition in party systems of different types. And Padgett had argued that the single-party system in Mexico could be considered democratic. Thus the solution would be: an empirical testing of *a priori* models of rational political action under different conditions of party competition, with Britain providing the case study of the two-party system, Weimar Germany that of a multi-party system, and Mexico that of the single-party democracy.

The logic of rational behavior under terms of two-party competition was fairly clear and indeed had become part of the folklore of the discipline: the system tends to equilibrium and moderation, with both parties concentrating their appeals on the uncommitted voters in the center of the spectrum of political opinion. In a multi-party system, on the other hand, parties tend to extremism, each trying to outbid possible rivals for the allegiance of a specific interest or opinion group.

But what were the dynamics of a single-party system? Surely the attempt to maintain the allegiance of groups with clashing interests could at best be only partially successful, opening the way for the growth of an opposition party or parties that capitalized on the resultant disaffection. Or perhaps the ruling party could maintain overwhelming support only so long as a relatively simple post-revolutionary economy did not generate a variety of socioeconomic groups with conflicting interests; but then its dominant position would necessarily be transitional, and a party that fostered economic development would be hastening the end of its period of dominance. Or perhaps the forces making for the growth of opposition parties could be contained by the counter-force of the fear of renewed civil war that might break out if political antagonisms were to grow too great; but again the assurance of long-term stability afforded by a dominant single party would in time surely cause this fear, too, to atrophy. Thus a democratic one-party system, while not necessarily a contradiction in terms, could only be a transitional phenomenon, its very success contributing to the erosion of the party's monopoly of power. Of course, the party leadership could always decide to hang on to power by hook or by crook, and a *non*-democratic system of single-party dominance might always be constructed; but if the system remained democratic, then it could be understood only as transitional, that is, only in a framework provided by the concept of political development.

The dissertation on party competition was never written. Samuel Beer tended to skepticism, and it soon became apparent that with the easy-going Socratic method followed by V. O. Key, the preliminary sketching of the proper manner of approach alone might take a year. But the decision-making system faced the problem of rising demands and diminishing resources: G.I. bill benefits were running out, and wife and child were increasingly dissatisfied with the marginality of a graduate student's situation in Cambridge. The dissertation topic became *The Relations of President and Cabinet in the Weimar Constitution,* which had already been the subject of a long term paper and an article;[3] and brief versions of what would have been the argument of each of the sections of the aborted dissertation were published separately.[4]

But the writer's perspective on the Mexican political system, which originated under those circumstances, and his belief that Latin American politics can profitably be understood in a developmental framework, have remained essentially the same, as readers of this book can readily see.

ACKNOWLEDGMENTS

The author wishes to thank for its support the Ford Foundation, through the research project on social revolution in Latin America headed by Edwin Lieuwen. He also wishes to express his gratitude to the friends and colleagues from whose discussion of some of the points covered here, and from whose assistance on his visits to Mexico, he has benefited; besides Professor Lieuwen, they are Marvin Alisky, Lawrence Alschuler, Pablo González Casanova, Roque González Salazar, Ivan Illich, Robert Cuba Jones, Dieter Koniecki, Manfred Mols, Rafael Segovia, Robert Shafer, Antonio Ugalde, and Luis Unikel Spector.

The book represents the author's thinking and, in part, writing on the problems of Mexican politics for the decade 1960-70. An earlier version of Chapter One appeared in the *American Political Science Review* for June 1961; a portion of Chapter Two formed part of an article published in *Current History* for January 1965; a version of Chapter Ten can be found in the pages of the *International Development Review* for March 1968; and Chapter Seven was originally published in the *American Anthropologist* of June 1971. The permission of each of these publications to reproduce that material here is acknowledged. In addition, Chapter Three is based on a paper prepared for the University of Michigan Faculty Seminar on Comparative Politics during 1963-64, and Chapter Eight on papers given to conferences on Urbanization in the United States-Mexican Border Area, at the University of Texas, El

Paso, and on Urbanization and Work in Developing Areas, at the College of the Virgin Islands, both in 1968. The paper given at the latter conference, which was sponsored by the Office of Social Rehabilitation, has been published in Arthur J. Field, ed., *City and Country in the Third World,* Cambridge: Schenkman Publishers, 1970.

Martin C. Needler

CONTENTS

TABLES

I. THE SINGLE-PARTY SYSTEM

Table 1
POLICY ORIENTATIONS OF PRESIDENTS OF MEXICO, 1917-70

Years in Office	Name	Policy Orientation
1917-20	Carranza	Conservative; but constitutional and legal groundwork laid for later reforms.
1920	de la Huerta	Provisional president for 6 months only.
1920-24	Obregón	Began agrarian reform, professionalization of military; pro-labor.
1924-28	Calles	Strongly pro-labor and anti-clerical; organized national bank, founded ruling party.
1928-30	Portes Gil	Provisional for 14 months; pro-agrarian reform, pro-labor.
1930-32	Ortiz Rubio	Conservative, weak; tried to stop agrarian reform; resigned.
1932-34	Rodríguez	Moderate; resumed agrarian reform.
1934-40	Cárdenas	Radical; strongly pro-labor, pro-agrarian; socialist, nationalist; reorganized ruling party; expropriated foreign petroleum interests.
1940-46	Avila Camacho	Moderate; effected reconciliation with Church; allied Mexico with U.S. during WWII.
1946-52	Alemán	Pro-business, developmentalist; pro-U.S.; economic growth, inflation, corruption; weakened agrarian reform; reorganized ruling party.
1952-58	Ruiz Cortines	Moderate, undynamic; continued Alemán policies in less extreme form.
1958-64	López Mateos	Judiciously radical; revived agrarian reform; pro-labor; "balanced" policies on business, foreign investment, relations with U.S.; greater scope for opposition.
1964-70	Díaz Ordaz	Moderate; continued López Mateos economic policies; harsh with opposition.

CHAPTER ONE

THE EVOLUTION
OF THE GOVERNING PARTY

As he was finishing his term as President of Mexico (1924-28) General Calles found himself in a difficult position. The candidate elected to succeed him, General Obregón, the most popular national figure (especially among the peasants) had been assassinated by a religious fanatic. A logical assumption, given Mexican history, was that President Calles would proclaim a national emergency, set aside the national constitution, and seek to perpetuate himself in office. In fact, many embittered partisans of Obregón charged that Calles had himself instigated the assassination with this aim in mind. No other national figure commanded the wide support of Obregón, and there was a very real danger that fighting would break out among partisans of the various presidential possibilities—as had occurred in the preceding two presidential election years. In this difficult situation, President Calles chose to seek a solution to the long-run problem as well as to the immediate crisis. In issuing a call for the founding of a political party that would embrace all forces sympathetic to the principles of the Revolution of 1910, Calles argued that the time had come for Mexico to pass from the era of personalities to the era of institutions, expressing his hope that in the future Mexican political life would be canalized in the forms of two-party competition prevalent in the stable democratic countries, with one party to represent the pro-Revolutionary forces, the other composed of those who rejected the Revolution.

Thus was founded the party that has ruled Mexico continously for over forty years; despite difficulties that confronted it in the early days, the party has faithfully complied with its mission of containing political conflict within acceptable bounds, of making possible the rule of impersonal institutions in place of the arbitrary authority of dominant personalities. By the same token, however, the Mexican political system has never transcended the problem implicit in President Calles's speech of September, 1928. A two-party system has meaning only if the possibility of an alternation of parties in power exists; if the progressive forces of Mexico were ready to pay the costs of a bloody revolution to transform the nation's social structure, will they be likely peacefully to hand back power to those representing a tradition other than that of the Revolution, if the latter should prove victorious at the polls? And without the alternation of parties in power, can democracy be maintained?

The "official" party of the Mexican Revolution, the Institutional Revolutionary Party (*Partido Revolucionario Institucional* or PRI), has ruled Mexico now for forty years, although in that period it has undergone drastic transformations in organization and changes in name. Until the emergence of a host of newly independent states in Africa and Asia, the PRI stood with the Turkish Republican Party as the only examples of dominant single parties functioning in an environment of relative freedom and civil liberties, and Mexico was and is commonly referred to as a "single-party democracy."

How has this situation come about? How does the system function today? What problems does it face, and how is it likely to meet them in the future? And what lessons can be learned from the Mexican case that might be of value for countries similarly situated?

I

The changes that have taken place in Mexico over the last forty years need to be set in a general context. We may begin with the reminder that the realm of politics is the realm of clashing interests and aspirations. What may be called the "style" of a country's politics is determined by the methods it usually uses for settling such conflicts. The most common of these methods can be arranged along a scale, from force to bargaining to administration and law enforcement. The degree of the internal stability of a political order may then be gauged from the proportion of its disputes that are solved by means which are nearer the "administration and law enforcement" end of the scale rather than toward the "force" end.

Where disputes are solved only by resort to force, no consensus exists between the contending parties. In a bargaining relationship the parties are at least committed to arriving at a resolution of their differences by peaceful means. Where a problem can be resolved by administrative techniques, the parties are in addition agreed, at least implicitly, on a set of norms which can be applied to the resolution of the dispute by a third party.

The shift toward the use of methods of political settlement normal for a more stable, higher-consensus society has been marked in Mexico. If we look, for example, at the succession of presidents that Mexico has had since the Revolution, a clear change has taken place in their characteristic skills.

The presidents of the early years of the Revolutionary regime were, of course, military leaders—Carranza, Obregón, Calles. At the end of Calles's term, the Revolutionary leadership had planned another term of office for Obregón, but, as was pointed out previously, he was assassinated between the election and the inauguration. At this juncture, Calles attempted to make the transition from "personalist" to "institutionalist" politics, as he put it. In other words, he proposed to pass to a system in which the president would not need himself to be the strongest military leader in the country, but could simply represent the Revolutionary leadership, which would be institutionalized as a political party. As Calles explained to a conference of army leaders, the new president would of course "seek orientation among the representative members of the revolutionary family."[1] The provisional president chosen, Emilio Portes Gil, was an able lawyer-politician, who performed very creditably during his brief tenure of office. The president elected to succeed him for the still unexpired remainder of Obregón's term, however—Pascual Ortiz Rubio— proved ineffectual and inconsistent. He was, in effect, "fired" by Calles, and the experiment in institutionalizing the Revolution was called off as Calles assumed the role of "Jefe Máximo." And when Calles fell from power, it was to be succeeded as the leader of the Revolution by another strong personality and military figure, Lázaro Cárdenas. However, with Cárdenas's successor, the task of institutionalization was resumed.

Although Avila Camacho was a general, it should be noted that he was not the "heroic leader" type, the well-known battlefield hero, as had been Obregón and Calles. He was a relatively junior general who had risen to become Minister of War through staff and administrative posts. Thus although a general, he should be regarded also as betokening the direction which change was to take.

A "heroic leader" type of general was indeed available in the person of Juan Andreu Almazán, but Almazán was denied the official nomination and ran as an opposition candidate. In an election marked by considerable violence, Almazán attracted a great deal of support—more than the official figures showed.[2]

By the end of Avila Camacho's term, after Mexico had experienced, during Cárdenas's "New Deal" and the Second World War, both considerable economic change and a heightened consciousness of national unity, the time again seemed ripe to make the transition to a civilian president. Avila Camacho chose as his successor another astute lawyer-politician, Miguel Alemán, who might thus be regarded as the functional—though certainly not the moral—equivalent of Portes Gil. Alemán, in turn, was succeeded by a president who was primarily an administrator, Adolfo Ruiz Cortines. The next president, Adolfo López Mateos, also a career administrator, was born after 1910, the first representative of the post-Revolutionary generation to wear the pesidential sash. Gustavo Díaz Ordaz, who succeeded López Mateos for the term 1964-70, was also a career administrator. This progression in the characteristic skills of the men who have become presidents is symbolic of the progress Mexico has made to a politics of stability.

A like transition in political skills has been found characteristic of other revolutions, widely disparate in other respects, which have lived to become institutionalized. For example, according to Feliks Gross, "The American Revolution kept its leaders during the period of consolidation, and the shift was away from military leaders and political philosophers to law-makers and administrators."[3]

Barrington Moore, Jr., has observed a similar phenomenon, albeit modified by obvious differences, take place in the Soviet Union: "The Party man has had to change from agitator to political administrator and give ground to both the engineer-administrator and the policeman."[4]

The Mexican type of development in dominant political skills appears, then, as might have been expected *a priori,* to be a tendency characteristic of the stabilization of a post-revolutionary situation.

II

It has been suggested that the principal mode of settlement of disputes in Mexico today is by "administration." What, then, is the nature of the consensus on the basis of which it is possible for the solutions of conflicts to be "administered?"

Put very briefly, it is this: the organized interests of the country, major and minor (with the exception of large-scale employers of labor) are integrated into the structure of the "official" government party, the PRI. These interest groups are currently organized into three "sectors" of the party—labor, agrarian, and "popular," the last a catchall category.[5] Major lines of party policy on public questions are subject to a process of bargaining and compromise among sector leaders, important political figures, and representatives of business interests.

From the point of view of the evolution of the Mexican political style, there are several things to be said about this sector organization of the party. First, it originated in an epoch in which the use of force was an ever-present possibility. For this reason, the three original sectors of the "official" party, when it was first constituted as the National Revolutionary Party, were those of the military, labor, and the agrarians (i.e., members of the *ejidos,* the landholding units established under the agrarian reform program); *for these three elements had "earned" their places by virtue of their capabilities as fighting forces.*[6] Given the possibility of violence, successful peaceful decision making required the participation of those groups able to use violence effectively.[7]

The organized beneficiaries of the land reform, the *ejidatarios,* and, to a lesser extent, organized labor, had demonstrated their fighting capabilities in enabling the government to survive revolts backed by major segments of the army during the 1920's.

Perhaps the most important of these—certainly the one which came closest to success—was led by Generals Sánchez, Estrada, and Maycotte in 1923, on behalf of the presidential aspirations of Adolfo de la Huerta. Disappointed by Obregón's choice of Calles to succeed him as president, these three major revolutionary figures gathered almost half of the army to their cause, which seemed likely to be victorious. But then unusual things began to happen; organized *ejidatarios* cut Estrada's communication lines, sabotaged his supplies, and even formed diminutive armies which attacked his rear. It soon became clear that Estrada's army was not going to be able to "hold" rural areas at all; and when President Obregón marshalled a new army out of the troops that had remained loyal, volunteers from the *ejidos,* and "labor battalions" of Mexico City union members, and took to the field, it was an already weakened Estrada he defeated. This marked the beginning of the atrophy of revolution as a Mexican institution, and thus labor and the *ejidatarios* strengthened their claim for an equal voice with the military in the councils of the Revolution.[8]

Much has been written about the Mexican land reform, i.e., the transfer of land from private or state ownership to *ejidos,* in which individuals have a right to farm a small plot of land without being able to alienate it; and a plausible case can be made for the view that other forms of agricultural ownership would be more productive—either outright collective farms, state farms, or straightforward individual ownership of units larger than the average small *ejido* plot. The fact that postwar governments have concentrated their efforts on opening up newly irrigated land to private ownership suggests that this view, that *ejidos* are relatively less productive, is the one now dominant in government circles.

But if the *ejido* system is not economically warranted, it is surely justifiable on political grounds. For the granting of land to the *campesino* was the one act which could secure his loyalty to the Revolution and assure that, in future revolts, he would support the government, and not, as had almost invariably been the case in pre-1923 Mexico, the insurgents.[9]

John Womack, Jr., describes the effects of Obregón's land policy in Morelos as follows:

> In return the local people were staunchly loyal to the federal government. When in December 1923 a revolt to make de la Huerta president broke out in several states, the country folk of Morelos kept their state quiet. . . . Probably not since the War of Intervention sixty years before had the allegiance of the pueblos to the national authorities been so immediate and so firm.[10]

As Obregón himself put it, "a progressive evolution has been slowly taking place . . . it is no longer possible to start a revolution in Mexico and immediately thereafter find popular support. . . . I feel strongly that this will be the last military rebellion in Mexico."[11]

III

The second significant aspect of the sectoral organization of the Revolutionary Party, for present purposes, relates to the political function of bribery, and "corruption" generally. For much of the period since the Revolution, and especially from about the mid-1920s to the mid-1940s, leaders and subleaders of the three great structures of power and interest within the party—labor, collective agriculture, and the army—have been so situated as to control the distribution of offices and their perquisites, licit and illicit. Operating under, at most, nominal control by those whose interests they are supposed to represent, sectoral leaders have been in the classic position of those who wield power without corresponding responsibility. As a result, purely personal benefits became counters in intra-party negotiations and the whole of Mexican politics bore a tinge of immorality and cynicism. In 1947, for example, Stephen S. Goodspeed noted the curious circumstance that "Army officers are associated with almost every governmental venture involving the spending of money."[12] On the labor leaders, Bertram Wolfe wrote:

> The writer has seen a list of his (the reference is to Lombardo Toledano, leader of the CTM, the Mexican Confederation of Labor) chief lieutenants, inherited from the past, with a price next to the name of each of them. The list is provided by the Chamber of Commerce of Mexico to trustworthy members to let them know how much it costs to settle a labor dispute.[13]

Thus the clashing gears of interest were lubricated by the heavy oil of graft; and though one can hardly condone the betrayal of his trust by an interest group representative, it should not be overlooked that in some ways the prevalence of graft-taking facilitated the transition to a more stable and orderly politics. Bribery has been known to perform similar functions, after all, in the eighteenth-century England of Fox and North; indeed, in the early United States of Alexander Hamilton.

We noted above that the *ejidatario* became a supporter of the *status quo* after he had acquired a material stake in it. In a comparable way, the trouble-making potentialities of the Revolutionary general could be inhibited by allowing him to engage in profitable if not altogether legal "business" activities. Those who benefit by the *status quo* are hardly likely to seek to overthrow it.

IV

The era of periodic revolts is over in Mexican politics; and the prevalence of graft has been reduced (though it has certainly not been eliminated) since the inauguration of Adolfo Ruiz Cortines as president in 1952.

In 1942, President Manuel Avila Camacho abolished the military section of the party as a separate entity. His successor, Miguel Alemán, pushed forward the development of the party sector into which the military was incorporated, the "popular" sector, which includes syndicates of groups of people as disparate as small agricultural proprietors and lottery ticket vendors, civil servants, and itinerant minstrels. With the atrophy of the military influence in Mexican politics,[14] sheer numbers have become of significance in lower level intra-party bargaining. That is, for example, there is a convention that the Chamber of Deputies seat in a district is assigned to the sector of the party with greatest strength in the district.

This principle has given an incentive to the sector organizations to conduct recruiting drives, since the more members the organization has, the more plausible will be its claims for a greater share of the spoils. And in order to recruit new members, the sector organizations try to find out what people want, and give it to them. At the same time, representation by sector enrolment has meant that the popular sector, which represents growing urban elements and is more frequently the majority sector in any one election district, has increased its legislative representation. The point should not be exaggerated. The legislature is an insignificant element in the political system, and legislative seats are not always assigned to the dominant sector locally. The increased predominance of the popular sector in legislative seats does, however, have at least symbolic significance, illustrating the tendency to moderation of the original Revolutionary fervor that has been growing within the party concomitant with Mexico's great economic growth of recent years—a tendency reflected in the moderate position of the presidents since Cárdenas. This development within the official party complements the trend outside it for an increasing share of the votes to go to the

Party of National Action (PAN), which represents in large part growing "bourgeois" elements.

v

Thus the style of Mexican politics over the last half-century has been undergoing steady modification. The emergence of a preponderance of force on the side of the Revolutionary *status quo* and the subsequent atrophy of violence were of crucial importance; graft and bribery had a role to perform; and the political effects of the land reform and of economic growth were significant.

The role of the official party has been, throughout the period of transition so far traversed, to contain dispute, to minimize the friction of change. The one-party system has striking achievements to its credit, which North Americans, trying to impose normative patterns familiar to themselves, generally overlook. Put briefly, the one-party system in Mexico has assured peaceful succession to power while allowing for a large measure of civil freedoms. In itself, this is a dual achievement worthy of note in Latin America. In addition, the system has permitted—indeed, has fostered—economic and political development.

Yet one must be wary of going to the other extreme, and of seeing the virtues of the system without acknowledging its faults. Mexico under the PRI is full of bossism, opportunism, favoritism, and careerism. Candidates are often imposed on the local party organization against its will. Brutal repression of dissent still occurs on occasion.

With all its advantages—by comparison with what went before in Mexico, with what would probably have occurred in Mexico without it, and with what has taken place elsewhere in Latin America—the one-party system, well suited though it has been to the politics of this transitional period in Mexican life, is itself a transitional form. The old arguments for a system of effective party competition, where a society can support it, are still good ones. And the models which ascribe properties of equilibrium to systems of two- or multi-party competition, but not of one-party dominance,[15] are still accurate. It is unlikely, to put it another way, that in a democratic and "developed" society a one-party system can persist. By its success in contributing to Mexico's development, the one-party system is making itself obsolete there. But it can hardly be denied that it performed its historical role well.

CHAPTER TWO

ELECTIONS IN A
ONE-PARTY SYSTEM

I

Ever since it was first organized in 1929, the present governing party of Mexico has won every election for president, governor, and senator. In this it has merely been following national tradition, however, since in the history of Mexico an opposition party has never won a presidential election.

The question immediately arises as to whether these elections are "rigged," and several observers seem to assume as a matter of course that Mexican elections are fraudulent.[1]

Today the typical picture is rather one of spontaneous violations of electoral honesty by some overenthusiastic local PRI partisans, but no deliberate national policy of rigging the elections. This does not mean that the national leadership would necessarily shrink from annulling an important election which was won by the opposition. This may have occurred with the Baja California local elections of 1968, which were annulled because of "irregularities" in the voting. It remains an open question whether the PRI would allow a victorious presidential candidate of the opposition to take office. In 1940, when an opposition victory appeared possible, the national leadership was divided on the question. According to Emilio Portes Gil, the incumbent president, Lázaro Cárdenas, was at first disposed to turn over power to the opposition candidate, Almazán, if he should win, but was finally persuaded to go along with the announcement of fraudulent voting returns.[2]

As it happened, Almazán did not gain a majority of the national vote, though he carried the Federal District.[3] In the last thirty years, however, no presidential election has been as close as that of 1940, no reason for "rigging" has arisen, and so the question of whether the PRI would allow itself to be voted out of national power must remain open; probably the national leadership does not know itself what it would do if the occasion arose. In the present situation, in which opposition candidates for the presidency present no real threat, only spontaneous local-level fraud of a minor character seems to mar presidential elections. But as Portes Gil writes, "In every electoral struggle it is impossible for the President to prevent low-ranking state authorities from intervening and violating the guarantees to which the candidates and their partisans have full right, and it would be unjust to make him responsible for such arbitrary acts."[4]

Despite the minor local-level fraud that still occurs, however, there is reason to believe that the official electoral figures do correspond, in most cases, to the voters' preferences. Thus the well-known survey of voter opinions conducted by Gabriel Almond and Sidney Verba shows a distribution of opinions similar to that given by the official voting figures.

In the presidential elections of 1958, the national vote for the opposition PAN was given by the official figures as 705,303, or 9.4 percent of the total vote cast.[5] State by state, the PAN vote varied from a little over 1 percent in the states of Mexico, Tlaxcala, and Tabasco to 39 percent in Baja California Norte, the PAN vote being higher in the more developed and more urban states.

The Almond and Verba sample of urban dwellers of the following year, 1959, showed 14 percent of respondents as identifiers with the PAN.[6] Seeing that Mexico's population is only about half urban, and there is less identification with PAN in rural areas, nationwide sympathy for the party must be somewhere between a maximum of 14 percent, if rural dwellers had the same proportion of PAN sympathizers as urbanites, and a minimum of half that figure, or 7 percent, if there were no *panistas* in the countryside. The median figure of 10.5 percent would probably be a generous estimate. Moreover, PAN identifiers are somewhat less likely to bother to vote than PRI supporters.[7] Thus the announced national vote for the PAN of 9.4 percent appears to be about what would be expected on the basis of the opinion survey data.[8] For 1958, at any rate, the announced voting results seem authentic.

It should be borne in mind, however, that the preference of the voters for the PRI is normally so great that the party loses nothing by reporting the vote accurately. Should this situation change, there will arise great temptation to revert to the practices of earlier days.

II

At the national level, however, no one doubts for a moment that the PRI candidate will be victorious no matter how scrupulously the vote is recorded. Yet if the outcome of the election is in effect known beforehand, why do people bother to vote?

The simplest and most obvious answer is that voting in Mexico is compulsory: the citizen who is not able to produce his voter's credential marked so as to certify that he has voted in the last election may find himself considered ineligible for a passport, or a driver's license, or to enroll his children in public school. However, it is possible, though a cumbersome procedure, to be excused obligatory voting retroactively for sickness or some other reason.

In the presidential elections of 1964 over 70 percent of the electorate—about 10 million of the 13.5 million registered—actually voted, and almost all those eligible to vote were actually registered.[9] In 1970 22.6 million were registered, but only 64 percent of these voted. The opposition, especially of students, claimed this as a success of their campaign for an election boycott, but the question was complicated by the fact that in 1970 eighteen-year-olds were eligible to vote for the first time.

An electoral boycott as a demonstration of opposition seems logical in Mexico. Voting in Mexico is considered an important civic duty and a tremendous campaign to bring out the vote is conducted by the political parties in all communications media. Thus to some extent voting in Mexico has the function of an affirmation of loyalty and a demonstration of group solidarity. This interpretation seems borne out by the fact that it is in areas with greater consciousness of social solidarity—the smaller towns and the less developed states[10]—that report a higher proportion of the population voting. Surveys in other countries have found that participation is higher in communities that are more homogeneous in social and economic status.[11]

It is worthy of note that the higher level of turnout in the less developed areas is not a function of the degree of competitiveness in the election, but rather the contrary. Barry Ames has found that, as a rule, the larger the PRI percentage of the vote (and thus the *smaller* the degree of competition), the larger the turnout.[12] In Mexico, as Pablo González Casanova has pointed out, competitiveness increases with the degree of economic development in the state.[13] Thus the findings of V. O. Key and others that participation increases with the degree of competitiveness of the election[14] are not evidenced by the Mexican data.

This function of electoral turnout as a demonstrator of group solidarity has also been noted by David E. Butler in British mining villages that overwhelmingly support the Labour Party.[15] According to Ronald H. McDonald, more traditional sectors of the Salvadorean population cast a pro-government vote as a ritual demonstration of solidarity.[16] The patterns of abstention and dissent in Mexico are also comparable in some ways to those described by

Jerome M. Gilison in the Soviet Union when he characterizes Soviet electoral behavior as group solidarity in the rural areas, and individual dissent and abstention in the cities.[17] The larger cities of Mexico show the existence of this dissent in electoral abstention and in lower rates of membership in the PRI.[18]

The different relation between competitiveness and participation should not be taken to mean that other regularities in voting behavior observed in the United States do not apply in Mexico. Thus, for example, when one controls for size of town of residence, then participation rises with the level of education, just as in the United States and Western Europe.[19] Since opposition to the PRI also rises with education,[20] one is presented with the interesting circumstance that the educational group most loyal to the PRI is that of Mexicans with primary education only. Those totally without schooling tend more to apathy and non-voting; those with secondary or university education tend more to support the parties of opposition.

On the basis of the evidence available to us, two rival hypotheses can explain equally well the higher degree of opposition to the PRI among voters with more schooling. It may be that opposition derives from some characteristic of education itself, such as greater sophistication, leading to a higher degree of perception of the shortcomings of the PRI; or it may be due to the fact that, normally, higher education implies higher socioeconomic status and the PRI presents itself consistently as a party of workers and peasants.

III

Although it is important to note the existence of dissent in the form of abstention and opposition voting, one should not lose sight of the fact that the PRI does after all win by overwhelming majorities. The question then arises, *Why* does the PRI always win?

One should start by acknowledging that the demonstration of solidarity described previously as constituting one of the functions of the act of voting in smaller towns and less developed areas is not of voting alone, but of voting for the PRI. As the party of the Mexican Revolution the PRI is in a position to draw partisan advantage from the myths that dominate Mexican political consciousness. Thus there is a very vague distinction—and in the minds of many voters no distinction at all—between patriotism and loyalty to the PRI. This identification of the party of the Revolution with the nation is dramatized in many ways. The leading opposition party, PAN, particularly objects to the use of the red, white, and green of the national flag by the PRI for its party colors (in which the party symbol is printed on the ballot for the benefit of illiterate voters). But one can readily see how an unsophisticated voter could identify patriotism with party loyalty when the leaders of the government that represent national sovereignty double as campaigners for the PRI, the national president is always a *priista,* and patriotic oratory and partisan exhortation draw upon the same lexicon.

But the party does not rely on this source of strength alone. Before a national election it conducts a saturation propaganda campaign for six to eight months. Every roadway, every mountainside, every wall—or so it seems—is covered with party slogans, party emblems, and the name of the presidential candidate.

It is clear, in addition, that the official party also benefits from its control of the vast patronage resources of government. In Mexico there is no merit system, so that all those holding government posts, and those who hope to secure them, stand to benefit from being noted party militants. At the same time, the economic impact of government is so great that similar considerations of personal advantage reinforce identification with the PRI in the private sector of the economy. *Ejidatarios* who want government credits try to ensure an overwhelming PRI victory in their district. Businessmen with an eye on government contracts or their public relations "image," unionized workers thinking of the next round of contract negotiations—all have their fortunes linked in some way with the PRI.

But beyond the "patriotic" vote for the PRI, and the opportunist vote for the PRI, it is clear that the PRI would still not win its majority so overwhelmingly and so consistently were it not that the policy of the PRI government does in fact represent on balance the policy preferences of the vast majority of Mexicans. Cárdenas ruled on the left and Alemán on the right; but Mexican presidents since Ruiz Cortines have made a point of steering a middle course between the polarities of opposed economic policy preferences, making an ideology out of the concept of political "balance"— balance between government and private enterprise, between capital and labor, between collective and individual rural property, between foreign investment and domestic control. Thus government in Mexico today represents a consolidation of demands of all social and economic sectors, rather than the acceptance of some and the denial of others. Business gets its subsidies and protective tariffs; organized labor gets its fringe benefits and its average annual 7-percent wage increase. The stringent anti-clerical laws of the 1920s remain on the books—but, on the other hand, they are not enforced. And so it goes. It would clearly be extremely difficult to maintain a policy of this type if the economy were not undergoing steady expansion; but in point of fact the economy does expand each year at a substantial rate that gives no sign of letting up.

One of the main reasons that the candidates of the PRI win elections, in other words, is that their party's policies are simply very popular.

IV

From what has been said it is clear that presidential elections in Mexico do not perform the classic function of deciding which party's candidate will assume the presidency, since everyone knows perfectly well beforehand which party will win. What functions, then, do elections serve for the Mexican political system?

The most important function is clearly to legitimize the new president's assumption of power, not only in the more obvious sense that the candidate did after all win the election and thus his legal mandate to assume power, but also in the sense that the overwhelming visible evidences of support for the government candidate, the massive press coverage of his campaign, the omnipresence of the party's propaganda on his behalf, serve to create the impression that the candidate is the natural, inevitable, and rightful president of Mexico.

But the election has other functions as well. The demonstration of the massive support for the PRI candidate has a cautionary effect on the opposition, indicating to them that extra-constitutional forms of opposition to the government are clearly doomed and that the only feasible strategy to follow is one of gradual accumulation of support over the years by constitutional methods.

In addition, the election processes constitute a potent instrument of citizen education. This is true not only for the voter but also the electoral officials. The electoral law currently in force provides for a supervisory committee of one representative of each recognized party at each polling place; if one added to this the election officials and the police or soldiers assigned to guard the polling station, one would arrive at the conclusion that at least one out of every twenty registered voters served in some electoral task at a presidential election. In fact, the appropriate proportion is closer to one out of thirty, since the opposition parties do not have the manpower to meet their quota of polling-place representatives. In rural areas and small towns, there are rarely representatives of the opposition parties, and the polls are not guarded. The number of people involved remains sizable, nevertheless.

The Mexicans themselves are very conscious of the civic indoctrination aspect of the election, and the conduct of the polling is generally regarded as a measure of Mexico's political maturity. Thus the fact that the 1964 elections went off without a single incident resulting in loss of life was regarded as a triumph for the nation's civic spirit.

The election of 1964 marked an advance in civic maturity in another respect as well. For the first time in Mexican history the defeated presidential candidate, José González Torres of the PAN, acknowledged that he had indeed been defeated and congratulated the winner, Gustavo Díaz Ordaz. This stands in marked contrast to traditional Mexican practice, which was for the loser to allege that the elections had been rigged in favor of the government candidate.

Thus the process of voting in Mexico, like other aspects of the political system, suggests the conclusion that political practice in Mexico has clearly been evolving to a politics of stable constitutional procedures. At the same time, the electoral system as it exists at the present shows all the earmarks of being adapted to a transitional stage of development, which means that it cannot yet be considered that of a mature democracy.

> Of course, we must be confident that such an original electoral method is only transitory, that it constitutes a transitional stage of a country in constant activity, and that we must fight in order to make substantial reforms in our appropriate laws, to change the one-party system and implant a genuinely democratic system, in accordance with the aspirations and interests of our people.[21]

CHAPTER THREE

OLIGARCHY AND
DEMOCRACY IN THE PRI

I

The *Partido Nacional Revolucionario* was begun by Calles as a federation of existing organizations—political parties, trade unions, and other bodies of various types. This made the party a fairly untidy association based partly on territorial and partly on federal principles, rather in the fashion of the present-day British Labour Party. In other words, membership was possible either through membership in a local party organization or through membership in a trade union or other body affiliated with the party.

In this phase of its development, the party was not an integrated organization, but an aggregation of groups dominated by prominent individuals—Revolutionary heroes, interest-group leaders, regional strongmen. Although the party as such subsequently developed an existence of its own, its original character as a loose alliance of regional, sectoral, and personalist leaders persists, and in fact explains more about what happens in Mexican politics than the party's formal organization chart.

In 1938, under the leadership of President Lázaro Cárdenas, the party was reorganized on a so-called "sectoral" basis. Under this system the party became explicitly a federation of four "sectors" of Revolutionary orientation: labor, agrarian, military, and "popular." The labor sector consisted of the affiliated trade unions; the agrarian sector was made up of the *ejidatarios,* those who had received land in a form of village communal ownership under the government's land reform program; the military sector was simply the armed forces of the republic, choosing representatives on the basis of the normal military command units; the "popular" sector was a catchall for groups not logically belonging in one of the other sectors, plus the civil service unions, which soon became the sector's center of gravity. To those who objected that he had brought the military into politics, Cárdenas replied, in a phrase that has often been quoted, that he had not brought the military into politics, but had simply recognized that they were already there—and had reduced their voice to one out of four.

The 1938 reorganization of the party had several significant aspects. The sectoral basis on which the party was constituted reflected the Marxist *ambiente* of the Popular Front era, with which Cárdenas strongly identified himself, in making social class identification explicit. The reorganization was also a technique used by Cárdenas to consolidate his personal ascendancy in the party after his break with Calles. It was accompanied by considerable turnover in party administrative personnel; it had already been preceded by the organization of a new labor federation under the control of a close associate of Cárdenas, Vicente Lombardo Toledano. The party also had its name changed from the PNR, the National Revolutionary Party, to the PRM, or the Party of the Mexican Revolution. Apart from underlining the fact that this was a new party, and marking the break with the old Calles days, the change in name was also designed to give expression to the powerful wave of nationalism sweeping the country, which had been given new impetus by the recent expropriation and nationalization of foreign oil companies.

The later modification of the path of the Revolution in a more bourgeois direction was likewise signalized by a change in name and a reorganization of the party structure. In 1946 the same convention of the party which nominated for the presidency Miguel Alemán, who turned out to be the most conservative president the Revolution had yet produced, also voted to reorganize and rename the party. On this occasion the party was given its present name, that of the Institutional Revolutionary Party, the intention being to mark the party's entering an era of maturity and stability. At the same time the decision was taken to limit the party's sectors to solely social and economic functions and to revert to the pre-1938 system under which nominations for public office were made by party subdivisions established on a territorial basis, and not on the basis of parity of sector representation. This move appears to have been directed against the labor sector, not, as might be thought, the military, which had already systematically been subordinated to civilian control by General-Presidents Obregón, Calles, Cárdenas, and finally Manuel Avila Camacho, the last general to become president of Mexico. In 1940, Avila Camacho had abolished the military sector of the party as such; military members of the party either took membership in the party sector with which they had been identified before entering the army, or, in most cases, entered the popular sector.

The 1946 de-emphasis of the role of the sectors reduced the influence of organized labor, logically complementing Alemán's subsequent strongly pro-business conduct as president. The leaders of the labor sector objected strongly to the proposed move, of course, and when it was finally carried over their objections, Lombardo Toledano resigned from the party to form his own political organization, the *Partido Popular* (PP), now the *Partido Popular Socialista*.

Lombardo's position within the party had already been weakened when his patron Cárdenas left the presidency, and during

World War II he had been diverted from Mexican affairs by his role as leader of the regional labor federation, *Confederación de Trabajadores de América Latina* (CTAL) . His departure from the ranks of the PRI was part of the worldwide ending of the wartime coalitions between reformists and the segment of the left that responded to Stalinist leadership occurring at the time. After four years of unhappy experimentation with the new system the objections of the labor and agrarian leaders won the day, and the party was reconstituted on a sectoral basis in 1950.

II

In the development of the Revolutionary Party, it is possible to discern four phases through which the party has passed, as its character has changed with changes in the locus of political power. These phases do not represent total changes in the party's character, and elements are carried over from each phase to the subsequent ones. The national president is always the dominant figure. But the character of the system changes with shifts in the political orientations of successive presidents and the consequent shifts in the locus of second-level power in the system.

Thus in its first phase the party was essentially an association of military, interest group, and regional leaders who each brought to it his personal strength and authority, dominated by the country's leading military *caudillo,* General Calles. Under Cárdenas, strenuous efforts were made to strengthen the position of workers and peasants in society and the economy, and power within the party during this second phase shifted somewhat to favor organizations representing these groups, united in a popular-front type of coalition of the "progressive" classes.

As the 1930s passed and as habits of party loyalty became more deeply entrenched, power shifted from the labor and agrarian sectors toward the central party organs and the party bureaucracy.

During this third phase this tendency was rationalized, in terms of party organization, by the building up of the popular sector of the party, a sector whose leading elements were lawyers and the civil service unions. With the continuation of the same tendency, in the fourth phase power has passed entirely outside of the formal party structure. Today second-level power is exercised by career politician-administrators who derive their importance from their positions in government and who are responsive to pressures from a variety of interests, perhaps the bulk of which are outside the party structure altogether. In the words of Manuel Moreno Sánchez, leader of the national legislature under the presidency of López Mateos, in *Excelsior,* the leading Mexico City daily,

> Every ruler who emerges from the party has to state that "he will govern for all," meaning by "all" both members of the party and their opponents. With this viewpoint, and with the intention of promoting peaceful relations, frequently the rulers dedicate themselves to cultivating the sectors that are by nature enemies of the revolutionary tendencies, and thus also of the party, so carefully that they come to abandon the latter and abdicate to the former.[1]

In an extreme view of the character of this stage of its development (a little too extreme for the writer's taste) the party has become primarily a machine for winning elections plus a mechanism for keeping pacified, by jobs, favors, oratory, and ritual acts, lower class elements that might otherwise be inclined to be restive because of the primarily business-oriented development policies of the government.

Viewed in this perspective, characteristics of the presidents since Cárdenas that are not usually emphasized are thrown into stronger relief. Each of the presidents who served between 1934 and 1958, that is, those who carried the party's organization from the first phase described above to the current fourth phase, had characteristics identifying them with the party's first phase, its era as a cartel of regional bosses and leaders of the heroic period of the Revolution. And, as was noted, this character of the party has endured as a sort of substructure on which the changes of party character introduced during the other phases have been built. But at the same time as each president could plausibly be identified with the classic period of the Revolution, each had since acquired or sought to acquire identification with newly emerging forces toward which he shifted the balance of power in party and government affairs. Thus Lázaro Cárdenas himself was of course an authentic hero of the Revolutionary battlefields. However, his self-identification was not with his former comrades-in-arms, but with poor peasants and urban workers, and it was on their behalf that he instituted the sectoral organization of the party.

Manuel Avila Camacho is an extremely interesting figure in this perspective. Although a general, he was junior in rank to many active possible candidates for the presidential nomination, and as a soldier had been a staff officer rather than a battlefield leader. As much as from his military rank, his legitimacy as a presidential candidate in terms of the premises of the organization of the Party in its first phase derived from the fact that his brother Maximino was political boss of the state of Puebla. As essentially a Ministry of War general and military bureaucrat, Avila Camacho's identification was not with the Revolutionary army but with the newly emergent professionalized army; he represented not the army of heroic battlefield leadership but the army that had one vote out of four as a sector of the official party. In terms of the balance of power within the party the role of Avila Camacho was to continue to contain the military, and to shift the balance away from the labor and agrarian sectors, by building up the "popular" sector of the party.

Miguel Alemán, similarly, had legitimacy and plausibility in terms of the regional-boss-and-heroic-leader substructure of the party. Himself the strong man of the state of Veracruz, he was also the son of a Revolutionary general of the same name. Alemán's vocation as president was to develop a new political constituency by accelerating the development of Mexican manufacturing and commerce, creating a powerful new business sector (although formally outside the party structure) whose representative he thereafter became. The tensions and conflicts created by Alemán's attempt to move the center of gravity of Revolutionary policies so far to the right made necessary a period of consolidation, recuperation, and calm in Mexican politics. Ruiz Cortines, the last president of this transitional period, was also an old Revolutionary, known as the incorruptible paymaster of Revolutionary armies. The triumph of Ruiz Cortines represented the victory of the career bureaucracy of which he was the leading member. This was a bureaucracy in the Mexican sense, in which a career in public service can include equally well appointed administrative positions and elective "political" posts as part of a single career ladder culminating in a cabinet position. The party substructure of regional bosses, sectoral interest group leaders, and a few surviving military heroes still exists, but since Ruiz Cortines the country has been managed, national policy has been set, and the presidency has been occupied by the career administrators.

III

As the economy and society of Mexico have developed and become more sophisticated, the character of rank-and-file membership in the party has undergone change. In all the phases through which the party has gone in its development the rank-and-file voter has been regarded as being *entregado,* "delivered" by the party's bosses, whether these were regional strongmen or sectoral leaders or charismatic figures. In the least developed parts of Mexico, states such as Oaxaca or Tlaxcala, this situation still applies, and almost unanimous votes are recorded for the PRI with unfailing regularity. But the development of the country has created a growing middle class, a more sophisticated urban working class, and an expanded number of university students. Oaxaca no longer typifies all of Mexico. To be sure, the growth of the popular sector of the party was supposed to reflect the growth of the middle class, but the representation of the middle class by popular sector organizations was always "virtual" rather than "real" representation; positions of leadership in the popular sector were simply convenient launching pads for professional politicians rather than affording an authentic channel for sophisticated new voices within the party. And in any case the popular sector now consists of marginal lower-class organizations more than those of the middle class, except for the government workers' union.

Quite clearly, by the end of the 1960s the circumstances that had given rise to the one-party system had changed. "The country has transcended those circumstances, but the PRI has not adjusted to the new conditions,"[2] in the words of Manuel Moreno Sánchez, who had been leader of the Senate during the administration of López Mateos. Under the Díaz Ordaz presidency Moreno Sánchez published several articles in *Excelsior* critical of the authoritarianism of the official party. These articles occasioned a great deal of interest; coming as they did from a high official of the López Mateos period they carried the implication that Díaz Ordaz had not continued the liberalization begun (though not completed) by his predecessor but had instead tried to put the clock back to a more authoritarian era.

Díaz Ordaz had been one of the most conservative members of the López Mateos cabinet and as Minister of the Interior (*Gobernación*) had shared responsibility with López Mateos for the repressive measures that were taken against strikes and demonstrations organized by Communist and pro-Communist elements. The choice of Díaz Ordaz as the party's presidential candidate presumably reflected in part the expectation that violence from the left under the prompting of Fidel Castro would be a major continuing problem in the years of his presidency. However, it was also expected that López Mateos would continue as an active force in Mexican politics, assuming leadership of the moderate left within the party. Shortly after he left office, however, López Mateos suffered a massive cerebral hemorrhage that left him totally incapacitated, so that the *lopezmateistas* were left leaderless and in a weak position to press for the continuation of the liberalizing tendencies of the first years of the López Mateos administration.

Thus for example López Mateos had been responsible for the amendment to the constitution which made provision for the election of party list representatives at large, in addition to the district representatives that composed the Chamber of Deputies. Under this provision a party gaining more than 2.5 percent of the vote nationally was entitled to five deputies, plus an additional deputy for each additional 0.5 percent of the vote, up to a maximum of twenty deputies. This was clearly designed to give the opposition a voice in the legislative process without the embarrassing and resented necessity of disqualifying elected PRI candidates to make way for some opposition deputies, the method followed previously. Under Díaz Ordaz, however, the law was interpreted so as to favor the minor satellite parties of the PRI (*Partido Popular Socialista,* PPS, and *Partido Auténtico de la Revolución Mexicana,* PARM) and to the disadvantage of the *Partido de Acción Nacional,* the major and most genuine opposition party. Furthermore, the maximum of twenty deputy seats that could be won under the provision for party list representation was construed so as to include the seats the party had already won in the district elections, rather than being in addition to them. The Popular Socialist Party and the Authentic Party of the Mexican Revolution, neither of which won the 2.5 percent of the vote necessary to qualify for representation, were nevertheless awarded ten and five seats, respectively, by the electoral tribunal "in keeping with the spirit of the constitution."

A further demonstration of the rejection by Díaz Ordaz of the liberalizing tendency represented by López Mateos and the *lopez-mateistas* occurred with the Massacre of Tlatelolco, the brutal repression by government forces of the student-led protest of November 1968. One of the students arrested after the demonstration and its repression made a "confession" in which several leading political figures were accused of being the intellectual authors of the student demonstrations; significantly, among their number was Humberto Romero, who had been private secretary to López Mateos.

During the administration of Díaz Ordaz the growing desire to participate effectively in party affairs expressed by the middle class and the students was steadily resisted by the central party machinery, which attempted to handle nominations in the sophisticated states of Sonora and Baja California Norte the same way they were taken care of in Oaxaca, that is, by dictation from the party central office. The revolt against the indifference showed by national party headquarters to local sentiment in imposing nominees without reference to local preferences led finally to election in 1967 of opposition mayors for the cities of Hermosillo, Sonora, and Mérida, Yucatán.

The growing middle-class challenge to the traditional practice of imposition from the top had not gone unnoticed, however. The first president of the party appointed by Díaz Ordaz, Carlos Madrazo, had attempted during his brief tenure of office to reinvigorate the party, provide for rank-and-file participation, and shift power away from the party's bosses. By maintaining careful records of party membership he had attempted to deflate the numbers of party members leaders could claim to represent, thus weakening the legitimacy of their position. He began a campaign to suppress the sectoral organization of the party, replacing it by organization along district lines, which would have had the effect of strengthening the character of the party as a membership organization and weakening its character as an alliance of pressure group leaders. But the most important of Madrazo's reforms was to introduce primary elections to pick the party's nominees for elective posts. Although put into effect only for local elections, the results of the experiment showed the party bosses only too clearly what its effect would be if it were more generally applied, and they combined to have Madrazo removed from office before he had served a year.[3]

It has also been argued that the primary elections were a failure because they introduced dissension into the party, that they were badly organized and involved fraud, and that in any case Madrazo only wanted to destroy the existing machines so that he could replace them with a machine loyal to himself that would prepare his way to the presidency.[4] It seems clear nevertheless that many things are wrong with the honesty, efficiency, and responsiveness of the PRI; that the classic way of attacking these problems is to provide methods of democratic accountability; and that any major reform is bound to stir opposition and require a period of adjustment. Although objections can legitimately be made to the manner in which the primary system was introduced and operated, it seems an eminently reasonable way of attempting to resolve the problems that existed and still exist.

Madrazo's attempted reforms bear a striking resemblance to the "good government" reform movement in U.S. municipalities around the turn of the century, which likewise attempted to eliminate boss rule and introduce primary elections. Like the municipal reform movements in the United States, Madrazo's reform program was also felt to be in the interest of the middle class as opposed to that of the working classes. The sectoral organization of the party does have the effect of strengthening the labor and agrarian segments since the sector leadership can claim to be speaking in the names of many who are enrolled in the PRI automatically as members of *ejidos* and unions. In a district-based individual-membership organization the middle class and students would participate more and would thus strengthen their position as opposed to the more apathetic workers and peasants. Thus to many people the reforms proposed by Madrazo seemed likely to swing the party toward the right, especially since the suppression of sectors and the reorganization of the party along territorial district lines had also been attempted by Miguel Alemán. Although Madrazo was removed from his position as party president, the forces he represents have not thereby been eliminated, but have in fact continued to grow in strength. Student demonstrations, with middle-class support, against the imposition from Mexico City of the party's candidate for governor of Sonora in 1967, led directly to the opposition PAN victory for the mayoralty of Hermosillo, the state capital, in the following year. It was these forces that erupted again in the student demonstrations in Mexico City in 1968, and when the demonstrations were brought to an end at Tlatelolco, it is significant that Madrazo, like Humberto Romero, was one of the people that the government tried to blame as instigators of the demonstrations.[5]

IV

Thus the Institutional Revolutionary Party finds itself today in a curious and in some ways paradoxical situation. Because of the policies pursued by the party, the country has undergone great social and economic development. Yet the changes in social structure growing out of that development have themselves undermined the function that the party has been performing in Mexican national life. The party has been playing a tutelary role, guiding the development of a society not yet ready for democracy. Now that that society is becoming ready for democracy, however, the party finds itself at a crossroads—in order to follow through on its mission of guiding development, it should now begin to reduce its tutelary role and redesign itself for the more modest task of being simply one party among several competing for the voters' favor, while its internal organization itself comes to reflect the democratic principles which have begun to permeate the society.

The alternative to the policy of continued development in the democratic direction is that of maintaining the dominant position of the PRI by the use of force. The forces of liberalism that have emerged with the country's development cannot be ignored or cowed like the peasants of the Mexico of yesterday. If political liberalism is not to be permitted to flower into a thoroughly competitive democratic regime, then force will increasingly have to be used. This was the direction taken under the administration of Díaz Ordaz. Some observers have argued that the *noche triste* at Tlatelolco and the repression of the student demonstrations during 1968 came about only because the government became desperate over the possibility that disorders would mar the Olympic Games to be held during the fall of 1968, and the hosting of the games had become a major symbol of Mexican maturity that had to go off successfully. But there had been other indications previously of the road that Díaz Ordaz had elected to follow, even apart from the dismissal of Madrazo. Earlier in the year, the state government had annulled the municipal elections in Baja California Norte, ostensibly because of irregularities committed; but it seems clear that the PAN would have won—perhaps did win—the mayoralties of Tijuana and Mexicali in fair elections. In other words, the line appeared to have become tougher since the previous year, when *panistas* had been allowed to take office as mayors in Hermosillo and Mérida.

In its development, Mexico had arrived at a crossroads. To continue in the same direction meant to move on to the free competitive society of Uruguay or Costa Rica. Díaz Ordaz chose instead to take a road that veered back in the direction of the sort of dictatorship with democratic window dressing one used to see in Nicaragua.

v

One of the ways to understand conceptually an institution that seems difficult to grasp as a whole is to compare it to other institutions that are more familiar. The PRI resembles in some respects the Communist Party of the Soviet Union in being organized formally as though the higher organs of the party were responsible to those below them, whereas in practice authority flows from top to bottom. In some ways too, the PRI resembles British political parties. In making possible membership not only through local party organizations based on a district system but also through trade unions and other organizations affiliated directly with the party, the PRI resembles the British Labour Party. The manner in which future presidents are selected—an elusive process in which the incumbent president consults with leaders of interest groups, former presidents, and distinguished party leaders—strongly resembles the British Conservative Party's procedures for choosing a Prime Minister when an incumbent Conservative Prime Minister resigns, as these existed before they were reformed in 1966 by Sir Alec Douglas-Home.

But the best foreign comparison is probably with the Democratic Party of the United States, North and South, in the Truman era. That is, the party is an alliance of bosses, some running welfare-state machines in the big cities, some exercising petty dictatorships in backward rural areas; of representatives of powerful interest groups—labor, farmers, and, less visible but also present, certain business interests; of liberal intellectuals and professionals, and rural ignoramuses. The whole is held together by professional politicians who set public policy from positions in the formal structure of government; the party as such does not determine policy, although the groups which compose the party have their influence on policy. There is corruption at some levels of the party and, at the local level, in the backward areas of the country, there is arbitrariness and occasional brutality; yet, despite everything, the national party is a force for democracy and progress.

Of course, in the United States the Truman era is no more and the day of the bosses is passing. The urban population is becoming too sophisticated to vote at the behest of the boss, and development is occurring even in the traditional rural areas of the South. James Michael Curley has had his last hurrah and Mayor Daley's last stand at the Chicago Convention of 1968 may have represented the winning of a battle but the loss of a war.

The Mayor Daleys of Mexico are also making their last stand, in the Tlatelolco Massacre and the annulment of the Baja California elections. But in Mexico the possibility that the last stand of the bosses may maintain itself for some time as a benign authoritarian state has historical and cultural factors working in its favor more than in the United States—which is not to say that the same outcome is not possible in the United States too.

II. GOVERNING MEXICO

CHAPTER FOUR

THE PRESIDENT
IN THE POLITICAL SYSTEM

I

Although the character of Mexican politics is largely determined by the existence of a single-party system, it seems clear that it is not the dominant party itself that runs Mexico.[1] This point has been stressed by Frank Brandenburg, who argues that if the party did in fact run Mexico, then government policy would follow a line considerably to the left of the one it has indeed pursued,[2] since the government is clearly sensitive to business interests not represented in the party. Rather than the official party *per se,* it is clear that in Mexico the leading political actor is the president. The political system is thus one of executivism rather than single-party rule.

It is worth noting the contrast here between the Mexican PRI and the Communist Party of the Soviet Union. As was noted in a previous chapter, party organization in the two countries has several points of similarity. In both cases the theory of party organization has it that power flows from the bottom of the pyramid of authority to the top, each party organ being elected by that lower, whereas in fact the relations of power flow in just the other way, from top to bottom. In the Soviet Union, however, it is the party

41

officials, and especially the party secretary, who set policy for the government organs at each level and who supervise the government's administrative performance. In Mexico, on the other hand, it is the chief executives—the president, governors, municipal presidents—who control the party organizations at each level.

Yet this executivism is not to be confused with traditional *caudillismo*, which has long been a characteristic feature of Latin American politics. *Caudillismo*, the dominant role of key personalities, depends on the personal characteristics and abilities of the individual *caudillo*, and he is looked to for leadership no matter whether or not he holds a formal government position. In the Mexican system of executivism, however, it is the person holding a given formal office who has the decisive role. Brandenburg has tried to treat the Mexican system as caudillistic by talking about the leadership of the country as exercised by the "head of the Revolutionary Family"—in other words, the dominant *caudillo*.[3] But this formulation misses the point that since the administration of President Cárdenas the constitutional president of Mexico is always *ipso facto* the "head of the Revolutionary Family."

Although the president is by far the dominant figure in the Mexican political system, he is not a total dictator but is subject to legal, technical, and political limits on his power.

The legal limits are of a minor nature only. In Mexico, as in other countries of Hispanic culture, great stress is laid on legal, as on other, forms. At the same time, the judiciary does have a certain amount of independence from the political organs of government, as González Casanova has shown. This independence is limited, but a certain area of autonomy does exist. "[T]he Supreme Court of Justice acts with a certain independence with relation to the Executive Power, and constitutes, on occasion, a brake on the acts of the President of the Republic or his collaborators."[4]

The technical limits of the president's power are more important. Obviously, the president cannot do everything and, as the size of the government's role has grown, greater and greater portions of the government have been removed from effective day-to-day control by the chief executive, with state governors and administrators of public economic agencies becoming increasingly autonomous.

The political limits on the president's power are of especial importance. The major interest groups and important figures in the country have an influence on policy, roughly in proportion to their capacity for causing trouble for the president. As is true of all modern governments, government policy in Mexico is made by a process of interaction between political leaders and pressure group leaders in which both sides try to work out a *modus vivendi* under which both will gain their objectives while continuing to cooperate. The threat of refusal to cooperate and of possible sabotage of a government's policy by an affected interest group, implicit or explicit, is serious because it is unlikely that a government policy could be implemented against the wishes of a major group without resort to violence.

In this context, the role of the legislature is minor and basically ceremonial and technical. That is, part of its role is modification of bills in the light of their probable efficacy, their technical feasibility, and their consistency with other laws already on the statute books; in this process, the opposition Partido de Acción Nacional also participates and has an effect, although of course this is not a very significant area. The legislature's ceremonial role is to act, not as a rubber stamp but more as an official seal on the documents that will become laws. In addition, the legislature performs some minor functions for the political system, in serving through its speeches as a medium of education of the politically conscious citizen and also as an instrument for the education and socialization of its own members.

Of course this is not a very exalted role for a legislature to play. However, it should be noted that in this respect the Mexican Congress does not differ so greatly from other legislative bodies in which party discipline exists and a clear majority obtains. Even in

the Mother of Parliaments herself, complaints are often voiced that
the individual member has no significance and that decisions are
all made beforehand by the party leadership; traditional German
parliamentarism evolved the expressive phrase "voting cattle" to
refer to members of the legislature. Nevertheless, it is clear that
the powerlessness of the Mexican Congress is in a class by itself.

Just as the president dominates within the structure of national
government, the national government dominates in relation to the
states. Yet here again we find there are limits on national government power. Over the years these limits have grown as the former
custom of federal intervention in state government through the
replacement of the governor has declined in recent years to the
point where under Díaz Ordaz only one governor was replaced
before the expiration of his term.

II

If the first principle of the operation of the Mexican political system is that of executive dominance, the second principle is that
of consultation among major interest groups to attempt to satisfy
their demands so far as this is consistent with satisfying the demands of others. The major groups collaborate with this system;
even though their wishes may not be fully met, nevertheless they
get more by going along than they would by attacking the system
from the outside. However, the president can be gently reminded
of his responsibilities by full page ads or demonstrations "in support of" his policies, in case it seems that the group is being
forgotten.

The official party as such does not take part in this process of
demand management, of consultation and semi-public interaction.
The party's first task is to serve to mobilize the population in
support of the government and its policies. It is thus reasonable to
consider the party as primarily a machine for winning elections[5]
but one should recall that there are also other times at which the

government needs to mobilize opinion in its favor, as witness the role of the party's mass organizations as a counterbalance to student groups during the demonstrations of late 1968. One might go further and say workers and peasants are sometimes mobilized in support of government policy contrary to their own interests, since recent Mexican governments have been pursuing policies favorable to business.[6] From this point of view the government party is not only a mechanism for mobilizing opinion but also one for keeping potentially antagonistic interests under control.

Yet the party can play its role of mobilizer of opinion only because opinion is already largely favorable to the government's performance, partly because of the attractiveness of government policy, that is, as the results of the success of the system of demand management described. It is also a result of the many personal services that are performed by the party and its subsidiary organizations for individual Mexicans, often as trivial as intervening with local authorities to secure the provision of municipal services or to urge clemency in a petty criminal case. At this level, the operations of the party strongly resemble those of a traditional local party machine in a large U.S. city.

The party also has a part to play, again at the level of personal services, in making possible the opportunism and careerism that secure the loyalty of Mexico's leadership elements to the system. The sinecures available, the opportunities to use power and influence and to promote private interests, the expense accounts, all serve to attach to the system those at the lower levels of leadership in the mass organizations.

More able and policy-oriented leaders are attracted to the system by the opportunities for significant job appointments afforded by the great career escalator. The "no reelection" principle means that key people are not frozen in their jobs forever but that new jobs are continually opening at the top, and therefore at every level of the hierarachy. The single-party system means that a career can be made of political appointment to policy positions without the fear of losing office when the opposition takes power. An able politician and administrator whose performance remains of high quality can expect to end his career in a cabinet or cabinet-level position.

But to get along one must go along; what this means is that in order to partake of the benefits of this system, not only as a rising politician but also as an interest-group representative or even an ordinary citizen who wants his interests to be taken into account, one must accept the principles of the system itself, and especially its first principle, the authority of the president. Every attempt is made to meet the demands of those who collaborate within the established framework, but police repression and persecution await those who go outside that framework by refusing to abide by the mechanisms of intra-party consultation and instead take issues to the streets, or who attack the president directly and personally. Within the system, the message reads, all things are possible; outside the system, nothing. Because of these characteristics, Rafael Segovia has classified the Mexican political system as an authoritarian regime, following the definition of Juan Linz.[7] This characterization seems a little harsh; it ignores the developmentalist ideology dominant in Mexico and also the restraining influence of such political norms as that of no reelection. At the same time, the Mexican political system probably falls short of meeting Edward Shils' definition of the "tutelary democracy."[8] The key characteristics of the tutelary democracy are a strong executive, a tolerated opposition, and the existence of the rule of law. But in Mexico the rule of law is not yet completely implanted.

III

In the attempt to impose order on the development of Mexican political life since the Revolution, it is tempting and indeed almost axiomatic to depict that development as a single-direction evolution toward economic improvement and political stability on a democratic basis. Most of what has been written in this book up to this point has been consistent with this approach.

However, it may be that an alternative explanation of political change in Mexico which imposes a different pattern on the data has greater explanatory and predictive power. This is the conception of Mexican development since the founding of the single Revolutionary Party as a pendulum swinging from right to left as the inclusiveness of the ruling party impelled it always to search for the middle way between the extremes. Such a pendulum pattern would array presidents in the manner depicted in the following figure.

Figure

PRESIDENTS AND POLICIES
THE PENDULUM EFFECT

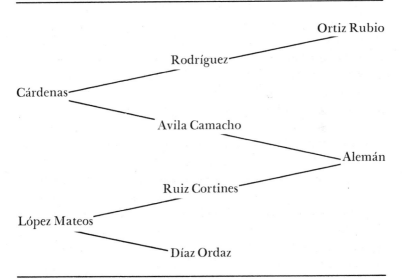

Note: For the presidents' periods of office and a brief discussion of their policies, see Table 1.

The pendulum starts out on the right with the first president selected after the founding of the party, Pascual Ortiz Rubio. He proved to be too conservative, especially when he tried to bring the agrarian reform program to a halt, and a sort of revolt took place against him when leading figures refused to serve in his cabinet. Ortiz Rubio was succeeded by the more moderate Abelardo Rodríguez, who was clearly more liberal than Ortiz Rubio on the critical agrarian question, resuming land distribution and denying the right of *amparo* to landowners being expropriated. Thus Rodrí-guez constituted a transitional figure as the pendulum swung back to the left under his successor Lázaro Cárdenas.

But Cárdenas was too far to the left in his agrarian and labor policies and was therefore succeeded by another moderate transi-tional figure, Avila Camacho. The pendulum continued to the right with Alemán, but the discontent aroused by his one-sided pro-business policies meant that the pendulum had again to begin its return trip with another moderate transitional figure, Ruiz Cortines. Under his successor, Adolfo López Mateos, the pendulum then swung as far to the left as it had gone since Cárdenas; López Mateos distributed more land than any president since Cárdenas, and introduced compulsory profit-sharing in industry. The result was that the pendulum began its return journey with the more moderate Díaz Ordaz.

The theory of the pendulum seems like a helpful way of describ-ing and analyzing the past. For such a theory to be plausible, of course, it has not only to provide a pattern for past events, but must also make that pattern explicable by asserting the existence of factors which cause it. This can be done quite reasonably[9] on the premise that a set of limits exists to the range within which policy is generally tolerable, the existence of these limits being demonstrated by the strength of the opposition to a given line of policy, by the difficulties of implementing it, and by the amount of disorder that it occasions.

However, the ultimate test of the validity of a theory is its power to predict. Various patterns can be imposed on the past retrospectively, but the one with the greatest explanatory power should also be able to indicate the direction of future events. If the limits of tolerability of a line of policy are indicated by the strength of the opposition to it and the disorder it provokes, then the point of furthest allowable swing of the pendulum to the right was surely reached under Díaz Ordaz with the Massacre of Tlatelolco. If the pendulum is working properly, then the presidential candidate chosen to succeed Díaz Ordaz, Luís Echeverría Alvarez, could be expected to take a more moderate position on questions of dissent and political freedom.

In fact this seemed likely, given Echeverría's prenomination reputation:

> Echeverría's candidacy will also profit if the party hierarchy decides to appease the elements disaffected by the brutal repression of last year's popular movement for democratic liberties; rumor and popular opinion have absolved the mute Secretary of the Interior of any real responsibility for the repression.[10]

Thus although the peculiar Mexican way of doing things has been put to severe test, and is likely to meet equally difficult trials in the years ahead, the mechanism appears still to be in running order.

CHAPTER FIVE

ECONOMIC POLICY

I

Economic policy has in most countries traditionally been a field of combat of ideologies, of conflict between grand alternatives based on opposing views of the world. However, more sophisticated approaches, based on a pragmatic refusal to view economic policy in ideological terms, have recently been gaining force in the developed countries, aided by improved techniques of data gathering and analysis.

In recent years the general line of economic policy in Mexico has consisted of an attempt to follow such a middle course between the grand alternatives propounded by rival ideologies. Since the end of the Alemán administration in 1952, Mexican presidents have operated on the principle of "balance," rejecting policies based on one ideological imperative or another. Fortunately, this policy has proved economically productive, as well as politically viable, thus generating the resources necessary to pursue programs that keep the major interest groups satisfied.

The classic issue of government economic policy is of course the question of *private enterprise versus government ownership and control* of industry. The Mexican economy has both capitalist and socialist features, and is in fact a rather good example of a modern mixed economy in its structure. Related to this issue, but distinct from it, is the question of *higher productivity versus social justice,* that is, whether government policy should, in the short run, aim primarily at raising the total product or rather at ensuring its more equal distribution. Under Cárdenas the stress had been on equality of distribution; the relative position of the peasants and workers in the economy improved but the economy as a whole failed to grow. An indefinite continuation of this policy would have led to the stagnation of the Mexican economy and possibly to a gradual deterioration in standards of living as population increased and as machinery became obsolete. Alemán, on the other hand, stressed the goal of higher production, and the gross national product grew as incentives for business were created. Profits rose sharply, but the lot of the average Mexican actually got worse as lower-class incomes did not keep pace with inflation. Since 1952 Mexican policy has tried to hold to a middle ground in which it is possible to maintain business incentives and profits but at the same time enable the real income of the popular sectors to rise steadily.

It is interesting to note that the various authors who argue that the economic advances made in Mexico in recent years have been made at the expense of the poorer classes cite data primarily from the Avila Camacho and Alemán periods, ignoring subsequent tendencies. The article by Oscar Lewis to this effect[1] is a case in point. Although still in print and widely cited, it was originally written in 1956 and revised around the end of 1958, being based on data only through the middle 1950s. Similarly the chapter by Moïsés González Navarro in a widely known book edited by Claudio Veliz,[2] first published in 1965 and issued as a paperback in 1969, cites data on this point only through 1955 and mentions no president subsequent to Ruiz Cortines. After examining the evidence as of 1962, Raymond Vernon concludes that "no solid support exists for the suspicion that Mexico's growth was largely a case of the rich growing richer while the real income of the poor declined. The rise of foodstuff consumption and decline of the infant death rate since 1940 suggest the opposite conclusion."[3]

The third great issue of economic policy, an issue which has assumed increasing importance in recent years in Latin America, is that of *economic nationalism versus integration into the world economy.* Although there are economic arguments for economic nationalism, its major justifications are political. Thus to the economic nationalist national self-respect dictates that a country be the master of its own economic destinies, rather than the passive subject of decisions made abroad or of fluctuations due to world market conditions. At the same time, of course, there are crucial economic advantages in participating in the international division of labor; and the most painless and effective mode of developing the national economy is to receive capital from abroad.[4] Here Mexico has worked out a complex compromise policy which seems to satisfy, at least in form, the requirements of both economic nationalism and economic internationalism. On foreign investment, Mexico leans more in the internationalist direction. However, tariff policy has tended more toward nationalism, a tendency which will have to be modified if Mexico continues to take an active role in the movement toward Latin American integration. This point is appreciated by the Mexican authorities and has been stressed in the policy statements of recent presidents.[5]

Under the government ownership phase of its mixed government-private enterprise system there is outright government ownership of slaughterhouses, electric power, petroleum, railroads, and the export and import of agricultural products. In addition there is government ownership in some areas in which private enterprises are also active, such as banks, iron and steel mills, and hospitals.

As in other countries of an intermediate stage of development, government-owned businesses are plagued with inefficiency, cor-

ruption, and political interference. Pemex, the government petroleum monopoly, can serve as an example (although it should be
noted that Pemex is something of a model operation as far as
state-owned oil companies are concerned; it does provide petroleum products to the consumer and it does make a profit). Pemex
employs between three and four times as many people as privately
owned oil companies of comparable size, while the strong union
influence on the company's management has led to corrupt practices. Examples of this become public knowledge from time to
time; for instance, in 1967 one petroleum union leader shot another
in a dispute over which of them would get kickbacks from the
thousand new employees who were to be hired at the Coatzacoalcos
petrochemical plant.[6]

II

It is generally known that a major phase of Mexico's policy of
economic nationalism is the so-called Mexicanization law, which
is usually described as stipulating that 51-percent of the stock in
any company must be owned by Mexicans. Although this is indeed
the basic norm of the Mexicanization system, the laws governing
the policy actually contain a complex mixture of provisions which
allow a great deal of latitude in the enforcement of the law. In this
respect, as in government regulation of the economy generally,
Mexican practice follows that of western European governments in
making possible highly flexible day-to-day government intervention in the economy rather than being episodic efforts to plan the
economy totally every few years.[7]

In practice, Mexicanization is mandated by law only in certain
basic industries, that is, in communications, transport, mining,
forestry, petrochemicals, banking, and publishing (and, for some
reason, in soft-drink bottling). In other industries it is not required,
but is encouraged by favorable tax and tariff regulations, and by

government loan policy. However, the implementation of the Mexicanization laws takes second place to the maintenance of a high
rate of investment. Thus, for example, the government tries to
avoid situations in which enforcement of the law means that a great
deal of capital leaves the country in a short period as foreign interests sell out to Mexican nationals.

However, there are variations from the basic norm in a nationalist, as well as an internationalist, direction. For example, in the
mining law of 1961 provision is made not only for 51-percent Mexican ownership of mining interests, but for 66-percent of national
ownership when the mining property is located on government
land. The provisions of the mining law are to be enforced fully in
the case of companies coming into Mexico for the first time; but already established companies have a transition period of twenty-five
years from the date of passage of the law for compliance, thus avoid-
ing the decapitalization problem.

Although the Mexicanization law was of course conceived along
economically nationalist lines, its effects are rather different from
those intended. It does serve to mobilize domestic capital and keep
it in the country by making available attractive opportunities in
association with well-known foreign companies. But provision for
51-percent control in Mexican hands does not necessarily mean that
Mexicans determine company policy. It is of course relatively easy
for a company to find a Mexican stooge who will own 2 percent of
the stock but will always vote with the foreign stockholders' representatives.[8] But in any case the well-known divorce between ownership and management in business today means that majority Mexican stockholding does not necessarily mean Mexican control.
This divorce between ownership and management is often explicitly acknowledged in the charters of foreign companies doing
business in Mexico. One provision sometimes encountered is a
stipulation that only a vote of 75-percent of the stock can override
management decisions. Currently becoming more common are

management contracts under which the foreign enterprise is entrusted with the management of the operation under stipulated terms regardless of where stock ownership lies.

This does not mean that the Mexican economy is being run by foreigners. Mexicanization does not ensure that direction of the national economy is in Mexican hands, because as far as individual businesses are concerned there are often ways around the Mexicanization provisions. But the role government plays in the Mexican economy, guiding, stimulating, and regulating every step of the way, means that even though an individual business may be under effective foreign control it can only function within a framework and on terms laid down by the Mexican government in keeping with the latter's conception of proper national policy. This illustrates the fundamental point that foreign economic interests can only dominate an economy where the country lacks a competent and public-interested government. This is a point often lost sight of in arguments over economic nationalism. It is true that foreign economic interests may bend government policy to their will, especially in the smaller countries. But most of the "bad examples" of economic imperialism occur when local governments have neither the will nor the capacity to manage the national economy in the public interest. This is certainly not the case in Mexico.

III

As far as labor is concerned, the record of Mexico is of a general climate of labor peace and steady advancement. During the first year of the Díaz Ordaz presidency, for example, the government's labor machinery conciliated 96.4-percent of the disputes on which strike notices were given, without a strike actually taking place. It should be noted, however, that only some 10-percent of Mexico's labor force of about 16 million is actually unionized. A little over a million workers are covered by collective contracts, which normally are of two years' duration. In recent years the norm has been for a wage increase averaging 7-percent or 8-percent per year to be reflected in each new biennial contract.

For workers not covered by collective contracts, that is, for the overwhelming bulk of the labor force, salary adjustments respond principally to increases in the legal minimum wage, although under conditions of labor surplus such as exist in Mexico many people are glad to get work at any wage and thus the minimum wage laws are only partially enforced.[9] The minimum wage is adjusted by legislation every two years, with an 8-percent annual increase being typical. Thus for those covered by collective contracts or receiving the minimum wage, these increases represent at least a maintenance and often an improvement of their relative position in the economy, since they more than compensate for the rise in the price level (averaging no more than 4 percent in recent years) and the increase in the per capita gross national product (up to 3-3½ percent).

In general, the level of wages in Mexico is one-fifth or one-fourth the level of wages in the United States.

For many Mexican workers, however, the share in Mexico's prosperity has been greater than the average. In 1963, the government of President López Mateos put into effect a profit-sharing law, under which businesses were required to distribute to workers a certain percentage of their net income after taxes. The percentage of profits to be distributed depended on the ratio of the firm's invested capital to the size of its labor force; the average proportion to be distributed was about 5-percent of net profits, the proportion running higher in the more modern industries. Enforcement of the law is not complete, especially where a plant is not unionized or has only a weak union, but implementation of the law is increasing. To the individual worker, his share of distributed profits can be a considerable amount relative to his wages. In the first years after the law was in effect, the practice was to pay workers their share of the profits in a lump sum once a year. Accordingly, most workers treated it as a windfall to be used for capital expenditures rather than daily living expenses, with a resultant stimulus in the market for consumer durables such as refrigerators and television sets.

It must always be remembered that the proportion of the population coming under the effective protection of the laws and practices described here, though growing, is less than the total, and that unionized workers are a minority of the whole labor force. Thus in Mexico, as in the rest of Latin America, organized labor cannot be thought of as a lower class; it is rather a more or less privileged elite element in the working class.

IV

One area of policy in which the tension between the demands of higher production and those of greater equality in distribution is particularly acute is that of agrarian policy. In brief, it has typically been assumed that a policy aimed purely at higher production should attempt to constitute the land in large farms worked with the latest techniques and machinery, while a policy aiming at equality should try to distribute the land in small plots to all those who wanted it. On this question, as on those dealing with labor and management, Alemán and Cárdenas pursued opposing, fairly extreme, policies, with Cárdenas representing the pro-distribution position and Alemán stressing production. Ruiz Cortines continued the Alemán approach, but under López Mateos and Díaz Ordaz the government followed with some success a dual policy of distributing land to the landless but at the same time encouraging the growth of medium and large modern farming units in areas of the country that do not have many claimants for land under the government's distribution program. These are, principally, formerly arid lands in the north of the country made arable as a result of government irrigation projects.

The basis of the government's land reform program is the *ejido*. This is a landholding community, sometimes not an actual but a fictitious community; that is, peasants may live in different villages but belong to the same *ejido*. Individual plots of land within the *ejido* are almost always farmed by individual families and can, since Calles's day, be inherited, but legally, at least, they cannot be bought, sold, or rented. The typical *ejido* plot is very small and located in the long-settled central part of Mexico. The collectivized landholdings producing hemp in Yucatán and wheat and cotton in the Laguna area in the northern part of the country are also called *ejidos,* but they are atypical.

The small size of the typical *ejido* plot does not necessarily indicate the standard of living of the *ejidatario,* however, since individual *ejidatarios* may also own or rent land or work as laborers on other people's lands in addition to working their *ejido* plots.

From the point of view of a policy of productivity it is possible to make powerful arguments against the institution of the *ejido*. Economies of scale are not possible on small holdings farmed individually, and the fact that the *ejido* plot cannot be mortgaged means that the *ejidatario* usually cannot raise the credit necessary for an efficient operation. *Ejidal* banks exist, but as it is difficult to recover loans made to *ejidatarios* without security, and as a certain amount of corruption pervades the operations of these banks, governments have been understandably reluctant to provide them with large amounts of funds.

At the same time, it should be noted that in a "social-account opportunity cost" sense, *ejido* production is cheaper than large-scale private production[10] in using more of abundant resources—labor—and less of scarce resources—land. Moreover, *ejidal* productivity has been rising due to more intensive use of the land.[11] But on the whole productivity does remain higher on the very small private plots.[12]

As opposed to outright private ownership, however, *ejido* property has the great advantage that it cannot be alienated, which means that it is not possible for a small group of peasants of greater ability or luck to reconcentrate land in their own hands and create again the problem of an overwhelming landless mass of peasants in the countryside.[13] Thus although there are economic arguments in favor of private ownership rather than *ejido* property, the political argument that the *ejido* system makes it possible to give land to a great number of people who want it and at the same time avoid reconcentration of land is quite persuasive.

It is true that in Mexico large estates still exist or have been re-created. Evasion of the land reform law has been made possible in some cases by the fictitious subdivision of a large estate among members of an extended family; according to one source, in the Valle del Yaqui 116,800 hectares of land, nominally owned by 1,191 individuals, are in reality controlled by only eighty-five landowners.[14] In other cases the law has been evaded by people with political influence, something that was made much easier by modifications in the land laws adopted under the presidency of Alemán. It is also true, however, that the government has been in recent years very sensitive to the charge that *latifundia* still exist in Mexico, and Díaz Ordaz has made a special point of expropriating large estates built up by people who had political influence during the Alemán administration. One observer wrote after the publication of the 1960 agricultural census, "Data on farms classified by size show quite clearly that the medium-sized farms are increasing in importance in the country, while the largest and the smallest sizes (under 5 hectares) are increasing more slowly than total farm number. This means also, of course, a gradual increase in distributive equity."[15]

The "balanced" agricultural policy followed currently is not a recent development that simply reflects the overall policy of balance followed by recent Mexican governments on questions of public policy generally. Viewed in perspective, the agrarian policies

of Alemán and, to some extent, those of Cárdenas can be regarded
as deviations from a single line of policy that has been followed by
the governing party since its founding, which was in turn based on
precedents of the 1920s.

The statutes of the *Partido Nacional Revolucionario,* written in
1929, make clear that policy was to be aimed not only at the distribution of land but also at an increase in agricultural production.
Efficient larger farmers were to receive government support, irrigation works were to be designed primarily to assist medium farmers, and the *ejidos* were intended as a way of liberating *peones* from
their condition of servitude.[16] These policies were reaffirmed by
President Ortiz Rubio in his State of the Union message of 1931,
when he made clear that the *ejidos* were designed primarily for
subsistence agriculture.[17] It thus appears to be incorrect to ascribe
the establishment of the *ejido* system as the subsistence sector of agriculture to Cárdenas as part of the leftist disregard of productivity
that characterized other aspects of Cárdenas's policies.[18] From this
perspective the "balanced" policies of López Mateos and Díaz
Ordaz represented not an innovation but a return to the original
spirit of the agrarian legislation.

The dual policy followed by the government has given Mexico
a landholding structure rather different from Latin American
norms. A much larger proportion of farming units in Mexico are
minifundios than the Latin American average; but a greater
proportion of farm production comes from the larger units—0.5-
percent of all units produce 32-percent of farm yield.[19] Compared
to Latin American norms, therefore, the picture is of a wider distribution of the land and greater efficiency in the large holdings re-
maining—essentially the original goals of agrarian policy.

What the original policy did not take into account, however,
was the growth in the rural population; in fact, in that era Mexico
was still thought of as an underpopulated country, with surplus
land available. According to one estimate, there are today 350,000

campesinos entitled to land who have not received it; landless laborers constitute half of the agricultural work force, and their numbers are growing.[20] The scarcity of land for distribution to those who want it is the core of the agrarian problem in Mexico today.

V

The major features of the Mexican economy are as follows:

1. A bifurcation exists between the traditional and modern sectors of the economy, with the traditional sector consisting essentially of the raising of food crops for consumption either by the producer or in the immediate vicinity, together with some handcrafts. A steadily diminishing proportion of the population is involved in the traditional sector.

2. The structure of the economy is changing. The relative importance of agriculture and mining is declining while the relative importance of manufacturing and commerce is rising. Despite this *relative* decline in the agricultural sector, agriculture is actually experiencing an increase of production in absolute terms. In fact, in the period 1930-60, Mexican farm production more than trebled, a very distinguished performance compared with that of other countries.[21] There is slow growth in such traditional food crops as corn and beans, but more rapid growth in such products of larger scale farming operations as coffee, wheat, cotton, and cattle.

3. The economy as a whole continues to grow steadily. The cyclical effects formerly associated with the rise and fall in government investment related to the length of the presidential term have now been substantially reduced, as a result of deliberate government policy initiated under López Mateos. Government policy now aims at a 6-percent annual increase, which was reached, on the average, during the 1950-63 period and exceeded slightly thereafter. Given an annual rate of population growth of about 3½-percent,

the 6-percent rate means fulfillment of the Alliance for Progress
goal of a 2½-percent increase in GNP per capita. (See Table 2 for

Table 2

Country	Annual Growth, %	
	GNP 1961-67	Population, 1970
Panama	8	3.2
Nicaragua	8	2.9
MEXICO	7	3.4
Costa Rica	6	3.8
El Salvador	6	3.3
Bolivia	6	2.4
Peru	6	3.1
Colombia	5	3.4
Chile	5	2.3
Ecuador	5	3.4
Guatemala	5	2.8
Honduras	5	3.4
Venezuela	5	3.3
Brazil	4	2.8
Paraguay	4	3.4
Dominican Republic	4	3.4
Argentina	2	1.5
Uruguay	1	1.2
Haiti	−2	2.4
Latin America	5	2.9

Source: Organization of American States, *Datos Básicos de Población en América Latina,* Washington, D.C., 1970.

comparison of Mexican with other Latin American countries'
GNP and population growth.) Even in poor years the rate of economic growth always exceeds the rate of population growth, so
there is always some improvement on a per capita basis.

4. One of the keys to Mexican growth is the high rate of invest-

ment, about 15-percent of the GNP during the 1960s. A substantial portion of the amount invested comes from abroad, and investment constitutes the leading single item in the government budget.

5. Nevertheless, government cannot ever relax in the pursuit of steady growth. At current levels, the rate of growth in population means that the economy must provide about half a million new jobs per year to take care of those joining the labor force.

6. Despite the high rates of growth and government investment, inflation has remained under control, with the annual increase in the price level averaging between 2-percent and 4-percent. The Mexican peso is freely convertible, and its international exchange value has remained constant since 1954; in fact it is used as a hard currency in World Bank transactions.

7. The tax system, long a traditional Latin American system based on a multitude of petty and often counter-productive exactions, is in process of modernization. By the beginning of the Díaz Ordaz administration the income tax had become the leading earner of revenue.

8. Attempts are being made to modify the traditional Hispanic systems of elaborate government regulation of the economy where these serve no economic purposes. Nevertheless, a cumbersome and counter-productive system of permits, licenses, and elaborate procedures continues to exist and to get in the way of economic efficiency.

9. The value of Mexico's exports is rising at 8.5-percent a year. This is close to the world rate of 8.9-percent, and considerably ahead of the Latin American average of 2.7-percent.

10. Exports are also diversifying. As recently as 1956, 70-percent of the total value of exports was derived from the sale of seven products. By 1965 it took the revenues from sale of the leading twenty-seven products to account for 70-percent of the value of exports. The traditional importance of the mining sector in exports continues, with the leading places being taken by silver, lead, and

zinc. But substantial growth has taken place in the export of agricultural products grown principally on large-scale mechanized farming operations—wheat, cotton, and coffee. In addition some manufactured goods are being exported to countries of the Latin American Free Trade Area, while about a third of export income is derived from tourist expenditures.

CHAPTER SIX

THE POLITICAL ROLE
OF THE MILITARY

It has now become an accepted feature of commentary on Mexican politics that the Mexican military no longer plays a significant political role.[1] Yet there are certain salient facts which seem to question the accuracy of the picture of a totally non-political military. Robert E. Scott concluded, in a work published in 1959, that "the military continues to wield a very important influence in policy-making."[2] Frank Brandenburg has pointed out that (until recently, at least) the president of the ruling party has usually been a career military officer.[3] In his annual *Informe* to the nation, the president goes out of his way to pay exaggerated tribute to the contribution made by the armed services to national objectives. Under President Cárdenas, the armed forces did for a while constitute one of the sectors of the ruling party. And in each "federal entity"— that is, the states, federal territories, and the Federal District—the military zone commander acts in coordination with the governor, both collaborating with him and serving as a check on his actions.[4]

Clearly, the formula that in Mexico the army is non-political constitutes a considerable simplification; what is required is a re-conceptualization of the political role of the military as a necessary part of the understanding of the total Mexican political system.

The first element in such a reformulation is an understanding of how the armed forces themselves conceive of their primary mission. The texts in use in military schools in the 1930s and '40s postulated the defense of the country from foreign threat as the primary concern of the armed forces.[5] At the time this was a not implausible position; tension with the United States over acts of the Cárdenas regime such as the expropriation of foreign oil companies made a United States invasion seem like a distinct possibility. Subsequently, Mexican shipping was sunk by German action, and Mexico entered World War II as an ally of the United States.

After the end of World War II, however, the possibility of foreign invasion became less and less plausible. To prepare for the defense of the national borders seemed neither feasible nor sensible: against Mexico's northern neighbor, the United States, defense is hardly possible; against her southern neighbor, Guatemala, defense is hardly necessary. As a result, military doctrine was modified, and the 1952 edition of the text on military ethics[6] lists the defense of the national territory as the army's third objective, with the preservation of internal order in first place.[7] This conception of mission is reflected not only in the training, but also in the size and equipment, of the armed forces. At its current strength of somewhat over 60,000, the Mexican armed forces have one of the lowest ratios of soldiers to population in Latin America and indeed in the world (see Table 3), and the budget for arms purchases is relatively small and makes no allowance for sophisticated modern weapons (see Table 4). Thus the line item for "Equipment" constitutes about 5 percent of military budgets, with most funds going for pay, pensions, and other personnel benefits.

The character of the army's mission is underlined by the fact that the militias of the *ejidos,* which played an important role in putting down the challenges to Revolutionary governments during the 1920s, have on paper been incorporated into the nation's

Table 3

MILITARY DATA FOR LATIN AMERICA, 1966

($U.S. AT CURRENT PRICES AND EXCHANGE RATES)

Country	Military Expenditures		Armed Forces	
	Millions of dollars	Percentage of GNP	Personnel (in thousands)	Percentage of population
Argentina	279	1.7	118	0.5
Bolivia	17	2.6	15	0.4
Brazil	798	3.1	220	0.3
Chile	113	2.3	46	0.5
Colombia	92	1.7	48	0.3
Costa Rica	3	0.5	0	0.0
Cuba	250*	5.0*	121	1.5
Dominican Republic	34	3.3	19	0.5
Ecuador	25	2.0	19	0.4
El Salvador	10	1.2	6	0.2
Guatemala	15	1.1	9	0.2
Haiti	8*	2.4*	5	0.1
Honduras	7	1.3	5	0.2
MEXICO	166	0.8	62	0.1
Nicaragua	9	1.5	7	0.4
Panama	1	0.1	3	0.2
Paraguay	8	1.7	11	0.5
Peru	83	2.3	50	0.4
Uruguay	26	1.6	17	0.6
Venezuela	182	2.3	30	0.3

*Rough estimate.

Source: U.S. Arms Control and Disarmament Agency, *World Military Expenditures and Related Data,* Research Report 68-52, December 1968.

military structure with the title of Rural Defense Forces. These forces number in size about twice the authorized strength of the regular military and are designated for duty only in their own local areas, thus constituting essentially a force for the defense of the interests of the *ejidos* themselves, and by extension the government they support, against internal threats.[8]

The second point to note is that national political ideology is

Table 4

MEXICAN MILITARY BUDGET, 1963-69

(IN MILLIONS OF PESOS)

Year	Defense Budget	Percentage of Total Budget	Salaries	Equipment
1963	1,485	10.76	688	108
1964	1,624	10.18	770	118
1965	1,910	10.70	917	121
1966	2,073	10.30	1,023	127
1967	2,148	9.71	1,079	129
1968	2,285	9.43	1,199	115
1969	2,548	9.61	1,299	140

Source: Secretaría de Hacienda y Crédito Público, *Presupuesto General de Egresos de la Federación,* 1963 through 1969.

clearly anti-militarist, in the sense that it assumes that military personnel will be dedicated to professional tasks and will leave politics to the politicians. This may be difficult to accept at first sight, given the history of Mexico, especially post-Revolutionary history, but it is well founded. There is clear evidence of resistance on the part of the military to the constitution by Cárdenas of the armed forces as a sector of the ruling party, and Avila Camacho dropped the experiment after it had been in effect only a few years.[9] An interesting and characteristic fact is that the leading present-day politician with a professional military background, Alfonso Corona del Rosal, who served as governor of the Federal District under Díaz Ordaz and was one of the likely candidates to succeed him, has asked the press that he be referred to by his civilian title of *licenciado,* rather than by his military rank.[10]

The political role of the military zone commanders should be interpreted in the light of this attitude. When the zone commanders take a prominent role in the political life of the locality, it is as agents of the civilian national political leadership, and not on their own account or on that of the armed forces as such.

In addition to the character of national political ideology and the definition of the military's mission, the armed forces are integrated into the political system in ways that are very characteristic of how the Mexican system functions, that is, through cooptation and the granting of individual benefits. This has meant a sort of preferential treatment of salary increases in the military. The norm of an annual 10-percent increase in pay has become established, and it is common for incoming presidents to award a larger than average increase or a bonus. López Mateos gave a year-end bonus equivalent to one month's pay immediately after taking office,[11] and there were above-average increases in the military budget in the first years of the presidential terms of both Alemán and Díaz Ordaz.[12] In addition, a comprehensive system of fringe benefits for the military includes pensions, medical treatment, housing, and schools for dependents.

This situation has made it possible for Mexican military budgets to be characterized in apparently contradictory ways. Most emphasized in the literature has probably been the fact that military allocations represent a declining percentage of the total government budget (see Tables 4 and 5). Other observers have emphasized the low level of military appropriations (relative to other Latin American countries) in relation to the GNP (see Table 3); this reflects the small size of the regular armed services and the fact that Mexico, not being involved in arms races with her neighbors, as are some of the larger South American countries, has not been a purchaser of expensive arms and equipment. Facts such as these can be cited in support of the thesis that Mexico is not a militarist country, which is perfectly true. At the same time, however, the annual rate of increase in military appropriations in Mexico, in absolute figures, is quite substantial,[13] fueled by the large increases in pay that are given annually.

For domestic political considerations, the fact of a high annual rate of increase in absolute terms is probably more important than the low level of total appropriations as a portion of the GNP, or

Table 5

Country	Pre-WWII	WWII	Early Postwar	1950s	Early 1960s
Argentina	18.2	30.7	30.7	19.9	16.0
Brazil	26.4	40.9	32.4	27.8	17.6
Costa Rica	7.7	11.0	9.5	4.9	4.4
Chile	21.5	27.4	20.7	18.9	10.7
Colombia	14.6	11.3	14.0	20.9	20.7
El Salvador	17.3	14.6	10.4	10.2	10.7
Guatemala	17.4	16.7	10.4	9.4	9.8
Haiti	21.6	24.0	21.4	16.2	23.5
Honduras	20.0	19.8	24.0	13.6	14.3
MEXICO	16.6	15.1	11.4	7.8	8.7
Peru	22.7	30.2	23.1	17.8	16.3
Venezuela	10.8	10.1	7.3	9.8	9.6

Source: Joseph E. Loftus, *Latin American Defense Expenditures, 1938-1965,*
    January 1968, p. 37.

their declining level at a percentage of the total budget. It seems
much more likely and more in keeping with everyday experiences
with respect to budgetary allocations that success in securing budgetary increases is measured by its relation to last year's performance in absolute money amounts rather than its relation to these
more sophisticated indicators.[14]

The other method by which the ruling groups in Mexico integrate the military into the ongoing political system is by providing
channels for individual political advancement outside the military
framework. It is very common for military men to be solicited as
candidates for elective office or for administrative positions.[15] In
Mexico there is no reason for a military officer with ambitions to
feel that the path to political advancement lies through barracks
intrigue and conspiracy.

Thus a general formulation of the political position of the

Mexican military has to be rather complex. Individual military officers may take active political roles, but this does not mean that the armed forces *as an institution* are an independent political factor. As an institution, the armed forces do serve a political function, conceived of as the maintenance of internal security, but this is a strictly subordinate role and not an autonomous one. That is, the armed forces as an institution do not contribute to the formulation of overall national policy. By Latin American norms, it should be noted, this must be considered a limited role.

A fair summary of the situation is provided by Lyle McAlister:

> Professional observers of the Mexican scene all agree that the armed forces are no longer a threat to political stability and constitutional government. . . . To assert, however, that the Mexican army no longer plays an overt or crisis role in the Mexican political system, or that it eschews a supermission, is not to say that it or its individual members are completely apolitical. . . . It retains vestiges of its position as a functional sector within the official party; it is a significant institutional interest group; and it is the armed defender of the revolutionary political system.[16]

Although the political significance of the Mexican military is limited, it should not be thought that this is an achievement for all time or that the military are forever precluded from assuming a more dominant position. Although the maintenance of internal order is a limited mission, it could nevertheless bring the armed forces into conflict with the national political leadership if disturbances broke out that the leadership did not repress vigorously for fear of the political consequences. Some observers have even speculated that the strongly repressive line taken by Díaz Ordaz toward the student demonstrations of 1968 was in part stimulated by the desire to preempt any military dissatisfaction with a softer attitude. In other Latin American countries, military assumptions of power have frequently been prompted by the feeling that incumbent governments were unable or unwilling to act with the necessary firmness to repress internal disorder.

Thus rather than regarding the achievement of civilian control in Mexico as a *definitive* accomplishment, it is probably wiser to think of it as provisional. In this respect, as in so many others, the Mexican political system must still be regarded as a transitional one.

III. MEXICAN SOCIETY AND CHARACTER

CHAPTER SEVEN

NATIONAL CHARACTER
AND POLITICS

What is distinctive about a country's politics clearly depends a great deal on what is distinctive in its history and in the development of its economic, social, and political institutions. At the same time, people's political behavior reflects to a great extent the imperatives that derive from leading traits of national psychology (understood, of course, not in a racist sense, but in the sense of the "culture and personality" school of anthropology). The implications of this national psychology for political behavior have begun to be explored by political scientists in recent years within the general framework of studies of "political culture."

Mexicans have long been preoccupied with the attempt to identify national personality traits, and a rich literature on the subject exists. As has been shown by Gordon Hewes and, more recently, Michael Maccoby,[1] there is a considerable amount of agreement among different authors on the nature of these leading character traits. The characteristics most commonly identified are as follows.[2] Typically, the Mexican is less concerned with the "external" world, and especially with its material aspects, and more concerned with the state of his soul. He conceives of the individual as relatively

75

powerless to affect the essentially arbitrary character of external reality, toward which a fatalistic attitude of resignation constitutes the best defense. People constitute part of this external reality too; they should not be trusted or depended on to excess. But the Mexican does not have too high an opinion of his own character either, extending to himself his generalized distrust of human nature. Thus self-absorption becomes self-pity and leads easily to apathy, sadness, and a preoccupation with death.[3] By way of compensation, the low esteem of the self is counteracted by an exaggerated self-assertion, and especially by an insistence on one's masculinity,[4] which in interpersonal relations takes the form of a persistent will to dominate. Thus in the Mexican are combined the Indian's fatalism and the proud self-assertion of the Spaniard to provide a conception of the world in which the individual must assert himself by struggling against an arbitrary external reality, even though the odds are heavily against him.

One of the ways in which these psychological characteristics become of political relevance is in shaping the Mexican's understanding of national history. The observer is struck, in analyzing popular conceptions, by the persistence of certain leading themes that are perceived as applying to the various periods of national history, themes that combine to form a pattern by which national history is structured. Basic to this pattern is the intervention in national affairs of powerful external forces which attempt to rule Mexico in their own interest. Mexicans resist these forces heroically; sometimes their resistance is temporarily successful, but (except, in some versions, in the current period of national life) resistance proves in the long run doomed to futility[5] either because of the superior force of the outsiders or because of the betrayal of national interests by some Mexicans who should have been loyal. This betrayal theme, likewise, is one of the constants of interpretation.

In this perspective, the conquest itself inaugurated the pattern, with the Spaniards cast in the role of the invaders from outside,

Cuauhtémoc as the embodiment of heroic but doomed resistance, and Cortés's mistress, La Malinche, as the arch-traitor. Padre Hidalgo, in his turn, led a heroic (but doomed) resistance to the Spanish masters of Mexico in the attempt to win national independence. When national independence was finally achieved, its democratic spirit was betrayed by the creole upper class led by Iturbide. Benito Juárez arose to lead the next incarnation of the Mexican resistance against the outsider, this time represented by the French intervention under Maximilian. In the short run Juárez was successful, but his liberal and national ideas were betrayed by his lieutenant Porfirio Díaz. Under Díaz, foreign interests again attempted to dominate Mexico, this time in the form of capitalist investors; the national resistance led by Francisco Madero was at first betrayed by elements following Huerta, but in the current period of history is being triumphantly vindicated.

Now it is perfectly true that this conception of Mexican history, the one that predominates in the national consciousness, is certainly consistent with itself and with the "facts."[6] Nevertheless, it is not the only interpretation of Mexican history that would accord with the facts. For example, one could equally well take the view that these various episodes were essentially unlike one another; that in the post-colonial period the conflict has rather been between Mexicans of different interests, with the role of foreigners only secondary. One could treat the attempt of the upper classes to re-create a Mexican empire with Maximilian as a perfectly understandable attempt to reintroduce law and order in the unsettled and chaotic state in which mid-nineteenth-century Mexico found itself, by the only means with which Mexico had had historical experience. Or one could regard Porfirio Díaz—as many in fact regarded him at the time[7]—as a farsighted patriot and stateman who, realizing that a liberal Mexico would inevitably be chaotic and turbulent, transcended his own early liberalism and attempted to develop Mexico by the only methods known to the economic and social sciences of his time, methods which are after all not too different from those used by developing countries today: that is, national planning and the importation of foreign capital and technical skills, while restraining popular drives to increase consumption. Or, finally, one could treat Mexican politics, from the Aztecs to today, as always dominated by a dictatorial government, removable only by violence, with self-interestedness and idealism distributed equally among authoritarians and rebels alike.

In other words, there are plausible ways of interpreting Mexican history quite different from those generally accepted. Clearly, the dominant mode of interpretation has political value for the incumbent regime and accords with its premises, but it is not an interpretation that has had to be forced on the Mexican people for crude purposes of indoctrination. It comes naturally—that is, it seems the most inherently plausible way of looking at national history.[8]

The present writer would argue that Mexicans find this conception of their national history most congenial because it conforms most with their psychologically determined conceptions of how the world is. In the words of Jorge Carrión, "The history of Mexico is full of stories which endure in it more because of their psychological value than because of the authenticity of their testimony."[9] In more exact terms, one would say that this conception of national history is formed by "externalization," that is, by the projection into the external world of the key forces active in the dynamics of the individual personality.[10] This is why the prevailing conception of national history emphasizes those elements which are also the main characteristics of the Mexican's view of the world and his relation to it: the arbitrary and alien character of the forces that move the world; the unreliability of human nature and the likelihood of betrayal; the need for the individual to assert himself in exaggerated form, to try to impose his will, even though the odds are against him.

For characteristics of this type to be so generally spread among the population as to shape national attitudes, it is clear that causative elements must be present widely in the patterns of home environment and early upbringing which obtain in Mexico. Such elements have indeed been reported frequently, centering especially around the crucial father-son relationship. Among the lower classes of the cities,[11] this typically takes the form, because of the presence of broken and serial marriages,[12] of a matrifocal household, with the absence of a stable father figure who can serve as a respected model on which the son can develop feelings of self-respect and confidence in the masculine role. Frequently a father is altogether absent;[13] probably most often the boy has known a succession of men occupying the father's position,[14] men who lack affection for him, whose demands on him and whose expectations of his behavior vary bewilderingly, and who, moreover, are rivals, rivals endowed with great power, for the attention of the mother. This situation clearly provides the basis for the perception of the outside world as arbitrary and indifferent;[15] of authority as brutal, inconsistent, and self-interested; and of the need to affirm one's masculinity in aggressive and assertive behavior.

In the village, the family is more stable, but the heavy demands and the insecurity of the struggle for existence absorb all the father's time and energy, meaning that demonstrations of paternal authority are intermittent and unsympathetic, and responsive more to the stresses of the father's life than to the behavior of the son.[16] "Parents often punish but hardly ever reward."[17] In this situation, too, authority is perceived as arbitrary and brutal, and only a weak basis for confidence in the masculine role is created.

It would be easy to conclude from this exposition that the Mexican case comes clearly under the heading of the well-known concept of "authoritarian personality," but such a conclusion, although true up to a point, would be misleading. This can be seen if one compares the authoritarian attitudes to which Mexican patterns of child rearing give rise with those typical of the German case. In the traditional authoritarian German family the father may have been unsympathetic and even brutal, but he was typically not "absent" or altogether arbitrary. The heavy-handed authority of the German father embodied itself typically in the demand that the child perform in accordance with an extremely exacting set of requirements, requirements extremely difficult to meet but which were in principle known beforehand. Because punishment was related to the failure to meet specific expectations, authority could be regarded as harsh and oppressive, but not necessarily as arbitrary or self-interested. Thus the typical "authoritarian personality" in Germany set aside his own needs in the fanatical performance of duty, duty conceived of as the self-denying compliance with a multitude of extremely exacting requirements, in public life, in private life, or in scholarship.

The Mexican situation is quite different. One cannot find satisfaction in the performance of what duty requires, since authority is conceived of as, by its nature, arbitrary and capricious;[18] one either commands or obeys in an anarchy of personal power, not in an ordered world of duty and regulations. Thus the Mexican is a rebel and a would-be dictator, not a fanatical cog in a state machine.

The conception of authority to which the early experiences of many Mexicans give rise, then, is carried over into conceptions of the holders of political power, both by those who are subject to it and, very often, by those who wield it. Thus the exercise of political power at less than the highest level in Mexico has traditionally been regarded in the sense of brutality, self-interest, and the demonstration of one's *machismo*.

These attitudes have been revealed directly by the use of sample surveys, as in the replies of Mexican respondents reported in *The Civic Culture*.[19] Most interestingly, however, the cynicism and alienation of Mexican respondents in this survey did not extend to two elements of the political system: the president himself, and the idea of the Mexican Revolution.[20] In the context of the foregoing analysis, the author would suggest that this is because the president, with whom the average Mexican has of course no direct contact, and who normally maintains himself above the daily hurly-burly of national politics, is regarded—so long as he plays his role properly—as an idealized father figure,[21] the kind of father that nobody had but everybody believes that fathers ought to be, that is, dignified but kind and friendly and concerned.[22] By the same token, the Revolution commands unquestioning loyalty because so many Mexicans can identify with it as the affirmation of the self against the treacherous, arbitrary, and exploitative power of those in authority and "the foreigners"—precisely the type of force against which the individual had to struggle in his own early family life.

As Mexico has modernized, structures of authority have developed which do not conform with the traditional pattern. There has begun to develop, especially at the national policy-making level, a body of pragmatic public servants doing an honest and competent job as policy makers and administrators, and this new style seems destined to spread. The public has nevertheless a long way to go before it can play the role of enlightened and self-respecting citizenry reserved for it in the modern political system that is evolving in Mexico. In this sense, the problem of the Revolutionary governments of Mexico is to develop, in both public servants and citizens, a conception of authority as rational, responsive, and sympathetic, which is in direct conflict with the attitudes inculcated by early socialization.

One key to the solution of this problem, as of other problems facing Mexico, may lie in the growth of the Mexican middle class, valuable in this sense not for its political or economic role as a class, but for its distinctive pattern of parent-child relations and the attitudes toward authority which they engender.

CHAPTER EIGHT

POLITICAL ASPECTS
OF URBANIZATION

One of the central features of the contemporary social landscape in Mexico is the rapid rate of growth of the country's cities. In 1940, there were fifty Mexican cities with populations over 15,000. In 1969, there were fifty cities with populations over 100,000; the number of cities over 15,000 had risen to 123.[1] Of course this growth has not affected all urban concentrations similarly; nor have the larger towns necessarily grown at the fastest rates.[2] Some towns—many mining towns, for example, or agricultural market-places—are growing very slowly. The boom towns are those which have a rapid-growth sector as one of the components of their economies: petroleum refining and shipping, or tourism and border transactions, for example. But the overall urbanizing tendency is clear.

According to recent estimates by the Inter-American Development Bank, Mexico's current rate of urban growth is among the three highest in the region. Although both urban and rural populations have increased sharply in Mexico, between 1950 and 1960 the rural population expanded at a rate of 1.6% per year while the urban population grew at an annual rate of

6.1% per year. The proportion of Mexico's population in cities of 10,000 or over over rose from 12% in 1900 to 38% in 1960; and it is estimated that by 1980, over 70% of the population will be classified as urban.[3]

Mexico shares with the other countries of Latin America this trend to rapid urbanization, which is much discussed in the area today. Obviously it has given rise to a variety of social and economic problems of a concrete kind. But urbanization has also raised political questions. What are the political attitudes of those who migrate to the cities? What will their effect on the political system be?

Drawing on impressionistic eyewitness experience, many observers of the Latin American scene have stressed the explosive possibilities of direct political action by the disaffected residents of the highly visible shantytowns built on marginal lands sometimes within but usually adjoining the city—the *favelas, callampas,* and so on.[4] The articles of this alarmist faith usually go something like this:

1. It is the more miserable, worse off, and worse educated people who come to the city from the rural areas, because of their inability to support themselves there.

2. They move from the countryside directly into the shantytowns.

3. The shantytowns are brutish and unpleasant places to live.

4. Their inhabitants are unemployed above the urban average.

5. The shantytown dwellers are without hope, unhappy, and alienated.

6. As a result, they are politically radical and ready material for revolutionary mass action.

Now this impressionistic picture is thoroughly misleading. In the first place, migrants to the cities are not the most miserable and marginal of the peasantry. Around 1960, migrants in Mexico had attained higher levels of schooling than non-migrant urban residents, with 68 percent having completed primary schooling or more.[5]

In the second place, new migrants do not generally settle in the marginal shantytowns initially;[6] many go to stay with relatives in older parts of the city, or move into the centrally located older slum buildings known in Mexico as *conventillos* or *vecindades*.[7] Those who do so make an adjustment, good or bad, to an already structured situation as individuals; they do not confront society collectively.

The move to a shantytown is thus commonly a step up for recent migrants who have spent some time in a central-city slum. Frequently, dwellers in shantytowns express themselves as satisfied with their new situation, which represents an improvement in their condition.[8] That this situation appears unsatisfactory to a North American observer is no reason to assume that residents in shantytowns are inevitably disaffected and alienated. Thus in his work on the *favelas,* Anthony Leeds has shown that many of their inhabitants fall rapidly into entrepreneurial roles and manage to get along rather well, in their own terms.[9]

Moreover, the extent of unemployment among migrants is about the same as among the city-born,[10] although in both cases many of the "employed" are actually severely underemployed.

It is thus highly questionable to assume that migrants as a whole, or dwellers in the shantytowns in particular, are particularly worse off than anyone else in the city, in material terms, either objectively or subjectively.

Perhaps it is still plausible to assume that a certain amount of anomie must necessarily be present among those migrants from rural areas who have exchanged a familiar environment for one less familiar and probably less secure, although survey data suggest that such anomie is in fact quite low.[11]

But it still does not follow that even those dwellers in the shantytowns who are alienated and disaffected will express their resentment of the situation in which they find themselves in political terms. They usually have a low awareness of the political system;[12] their time and energies are absorbed in the daily struggle for existence and leave no surplus for political involvement; and the settlements are normally physically removed from the center of the city where symbolical political acts take place and where protest demonstrations have most effect. Moreover, the slum dweller typically thinks of politics in terms of short-range material gratification and responds to personalist and nationalist, rather than revolutionary ideological, appeals.[13]

At the same time, it would be foolish to argue that there is never any revolutionary potential in the new settlements. An adverse change in the general level of economic conditions can frustrate the rising aspirations of even the most vigorous shantytown entrepreneur, thus creating the classic revolutionary situation. And the initial outbreak of revolutionary violence can occur elsewhere in society, penetrating the consciousness of even the normally least political shantytown dweller and making possible his mobilization into revolutionary activity. José Moreno has shown, for example, that although they did not participate in politics before the fighting broke out or join in the fighting right away, it was young residents of the *barrios altos,* the shantytowns of Santo Domingo's *Ciudad Nueva,* who came to play the major role on the Constitutionalist side during the later phases of the Dominican civil war of 1965.[14]

Although there are thus many factors which militate against the newly urbanized poor's forming a focus of mass revolutionary activity, such a possibility cannot altogether be ruled out. But in the Mexican context there is an additional force working to integrate the newly urbanized into the political system in supportive roles, and that is the government party, the *Partido Revolucionario Institucional.* One should bear in mind that the reason for the organization of the "official party" in the first place was precisely to limit violence in the political system by providing a mechanism for the representation of interests and the satisfaction of demands.[15]

The PRI plays somewhat the same role with respect to the newly urbanized that was played by the urban political machines in the northern United States with respect to new immigrants in the late nineteenth century. That is, party politicians make the cause of the poor their own, intervening with the bureaucracy to secure jobs or licenses, to arrange bail, to clarify title to plots of land, and so on. This traditional machine-politics approach of the PRI to integrating the newly urbanized lower classes by a policy of favors and handouts is particularly well suited to the situation. As was mentioned, political attitudes among the urban poor are oriented especially to immediate material gratification, rather than to questions of ideology or program. But the PRI takes a special interest in the problems of the poor as a class, as well as the problems of poor individuals. According to Antonio Ugalde, the attempt to improve the living conditions of the poor is one of the major activities of the PRI in Ensenada.[16] Thus the expression of the demands of the poor becomes a mechanism for tying them in to the government party, rather than a vehicle of opposition sentiment. The PRI, always on the lookout for unaffiliated groups of potential supporters, has recognized the urban poor in its characteristic fashion by establishing organizations affiliated with one of the sectors of the party to represent their interests: the *Ligas para la Defensa del Consumidor,* and the *Federaciones de Colonias Proletarias,* which are included in the federation of organizations that comprises the "popular" sector of the party.

That this strategy seems to be successful is indicated by the voting records of the cities. It is true that the opposition to the PRI is stronger in the cities and the more developed areas of the country. Thus, to take a typical example, in the legislative elections of 1961 the opposition parties won 35.32 percent of the vote in the Federal District and 33.01 percent in Lower California North, but less than 1 percent in the states of Chiapas and Tlaxcala.[17] However, the growth in the opposition vote has been almost entirely on the part of the *Partido de Acción Nacional,* which represents primarily middle-class elements and whose program consists principally of the argument "we could do the same things better" rather than the espousal of major changes in present policies. The comparable party to the left of the PRI, the Popular Socialists, which tries to be more radical and more "proletarian," has had virtually no success in recruiting urban voters. This suggests that the PRI has thus far managed to channel the demands of the newly urbanized lower classes in ways that can be contained without difficulty within the operating political system. For whatever reason, the percentage of migrants voting for opposition candidates was lower in 1958 than the comparable percentage of the city-born.[18]

There has been violent direct action recently on the part of the poor, led by politicians to the left of the governing party, but this has been confined to the rural areas, where it has taken the form of land occupations, or *paracaidismo.* Recent urban political violence in Mexico, such as the disturbances over the gubernatorial nomination in Sonora in 1967, and the Mexico City demonstrations of 1968, on the other hand, have been the work not of the poor or the shantytown dwellers but of the university students.

Another set of relations between the processes of urbanization and the political system lies at a different level. Viewed in developmental perspective, Mexico is a country which is trying to progress from a political system operating on the basis of the use of force and of favoritism, personal connections, and an obedient population, to one based on honest government, responsiveness to popular needs, and civic participation. At present in a transitional stage, Mexico clearly has quite a way to go to reach the second pole of the continuum.

Change in this dimension presupposes the modification of institutions, behavior, and popular attitudes.[19] However, the generalizations about Mexican character and behavior most generally accepted posit characteristics appropriate to the traditional authoritarian pole of the development continuum. That is, observers have stressed an image of authority as essentially arbitrary and self-interested, which means not only that the population has difficulty in playing the role of democratic citizen reserved for it in a politically developed Mexico, but also that those placed in authority are likely to fall into a pattern of abuse of power.[20]

Unfortunately, it may be the case that urbanization reinforces these inappropriate attitudes rather than modifying them.[21] Statistics indicate that for Mexico, as for other countries, lower-class urbanization is accompanied by social disorganization, the weakening of family ties, the absence of a male head of household or the succession of various temporary occupants of this role, higher rates of juvenile delinquency, and so on.[22] In other words, the lack of stability in the family and of continuity in the father's role is likely to reinforce the tendency for authority to be conceived of by the growing child as unstable, arbitrary, and self-interested. Accordingly, to the extent that the urban lower classes constitute a key population element, it may well be in the area of democratic civic attitudes—again, on the part of both citizens and occupants of minor positions of authority—that Mexico will continue to find its greatest bottleneck to the achievement of full political development.

Under this set of circumstances, it is worthy of note that the opposition party of middle-class orientation, the *Partido de Acción Nacional,* has made the achievement of the norms of good citizenship part of its program.[23] Originally a party of fairly violent opposition of principle in the Mexican tradition, glorifying premodern values and the Hispanic tradition, and condoning the use of violence, the PAN has now evolved to the position of a loyal opposition party.[24] The PAN presidential candidate in the 1964 election, José González Torres, acknowledged that he had been defeated fairly and sent his congratulations to the winner—something new in Mexican politics. The party has abandoned its stance of total rejection of the goals of the Mexican Revolution, which it now "accepts," focusing its opposition on questions such as honesty and responsibility in the public administration and in the electoral process. Clearly these elements in the PAN program are self-serving, and not just disinterested advocacy of good government: PAN urges the purity of the electoral process, implying that it does better electorally than the official figures show; it argues that municipal autonomy be respected, which is hardly disinterested since the party controls some municipal governments but not the central government; it attacks corruption by federal officeholders, none of whom come from its ranks; and so on.

It is nevertheless significant that this more modern civic-minded approach to the role of opposition has been taken, rather than that of a traditional violent opposition of principle. In this respect, the new orientation of the PAN appears indicative of the character of the new urban middle classes that it especially represents.

At the same time, similar tendencies affect the PRI. A body of "reform" opinion has been growing within the official party demanding an end to bossism and greater rank-and-file participation, and the question was resolved only temporarily by the removal of the spokesman for this tendency, Carlos Madrazo, after less than a year as party president. The desertion of large numbers of PRI voters to the PAN over the "bossism" issue, which gave PAN the mayoralty of Hermosillo in 1967, has made clear that something must be done about middle-class reform sentiment if the party wants to maintain its monopoly of power without continually having to resort to force.

The significant political issues affecting the stability of the system that grow out of Mexico's urbanization, despite the alarmism of the "revolt in the shantytowns" school of thought, thus derive not from the alienation of the poor but from the will of the better off to participate.

CHAPTER NINE

DEVELOPMENT
AND SOCIETY

I

To speak of urbanization, as in the previous chapter, is of course
only to abstract one aspect from a whole process of demographic
change. More precisely stated, these changes consist of: rural-urban
migration proper; migration from smaller towns to larger cities;[1]
and migration from the poorer to the more prosperous sections of
the country, especially to areas along the border with the United
States.[2] In the Mexican context, therefore, this whole set of demographic shifts signifies movement from the more traditional sector
to the more modern. The gap bridged by such movement is especially great in Mexico, since the traditional sector is in many cultural respects strongly Indian. The difference between the two
sectors, accordingly, extends not only to questions of occupation,
standard of living, and beliefs and attitudes, but also to types of
food consumed, styles of life, and even language spoken. In recog-
nition of this fact, the Mexican census tries to elicit information
about cultural style by asking respondents if they habitually eat
wheat bread or corn tortillas, wear shoes or go barefoot, sleep on

the floor or on a hammock or in a bed, and speak Spanish or an indigenous language.

Although the patterns of migration referred to document the movement from the traditional to the modern sector, such migration falls short of draining off people equal in numbers to the increase in population in the traditional sector. This has been pointed out in a careful analysis published rcently by the perceptive Mexican political scientist, Pablo González Casanova.[3] Thus the number of people speaking indigenous languages has shown an *increase* over the period up to 1960, as have the numbers of people in other categories which define what González Casanova calls "marginal Mexico" (see Table 6). A disturbing picture is created if

Table 6

TRENDS IN "MARGINAL" POPULATION IN MEXICO

(IN THOUSANDS)

Year	Rural	School-age children not in school	Not using shoes	Speaking primarily or exclusively an Indian language
1930	11,010	1,690		2,250
1940	12,760	2,550	9,850	2,490
1950	14,810	2,970	11,410	2,450
1960	17,220	3,120	12,740	3,030

Source: Pablo González Casanova, *La democracia en México,* Chapter 5.

one combines these figures on the increase in the number of "marginal Mexicans" with figures indicating that the benefits of the country's economic growth are being channeled disproportionately into the modern sector.[4] It becomes clear that the gap between traditional and modern Mexico is growing, even while the number of people in the traditional sector is increasing. At the same time, the marginal Mexicans are not effectively organized for political action, either in pressure groups or in subsidiary organs of the governing party, and so lack the means to redress the social and economic imbalance that grows greater as time passes.

While this picture is a disquieting one, there are two mitigating factors which should be borne in mind. The more obvious point is that although "marginal Mexico" appears to be growing in *absolute* size, its rate of growth is nevertheless much lower than the rate of growth in total population. Accordingly, the marginal Mexicans represent a steadily decreasing *proportion* of the total population. This helps to place the problem in proper perspective.

More importantly, perhaps, one should point out that it is clearly impermissible to extrapolate the gap in standard of living between the two sectors into the indefinite future. There is no reason to assume that the present directions and magnitudes of change will continue forever—in fact, there are good reasons to believe they will not.[5] By its nature, development does not occur evenly throughout a society in its initial stages, but rather focuses in the most favorable zones, these being in the Mexican case the national capital, the largest cities, and the areas closer to the United States border. After a certain stage is reached, however, development typically begins to spread to zones whose comparative advantage in factors such as lower tax and wage rates exceeds the "external economies" available in the more developed areas, and differential rates of development shift as a certain amount of "catching up" takes place. Some of these effects have been observed, for example, in the U.S. South in recent years, and appear to be beginning in the Brazilian Northeast, long regarded as an area hopelessly doomed to perpetual backwardness.

However, an important point is that the "catching up" process depends in part on government action in establishing favorable tax conditions, regional development programs, and the like. Thus although one may have faith that the process will eventually take place, for it to occur it is first necessary to draw attention to the existence of regional imbalance and agitate for its alleviation. Accordingly, the statement of the problem by González Casanova is of prime importance and is a necessary first step in remedial action.

II

To what extent does Mexico, as a developing country, have social characteristics in common with the other countries of the "Third World?" In his recent book, *Sociología de la modernización,*[6] Gino Germani has listed eleven traits typical of such countries. These are, in summary form, as follows:

1. The population explosion.
2. Rapid urbanization.
3. The persistence of archaic social patterns in the rural areas.
4. The existence of disequilibria among the regions of the country.
5. The phenomenon of marginality of part of the population, that is, its not sharing in the patterns and norms that characterize the national society.
6. The existence of a tertiary, or service, sector of the economy much too large with relation to the primary and secondary sectors.
7. Aspirations to modern consumption patterns, despite archaic patterns of production.
8. Retardation in the development of modern attitudes.
9. The simultaneous arrival of social processes which were sequential in the classic modernization patterns of Western Europe.
10. Political and social mobilization occurring earlier and at faster rates than economic development.
11. The persistence of military intervention.

Clearly, Mexico shares many of these characteristics—the population and urban explosions, the over-large tertiary sector, the persistence of internal disequilibria, the retardation in the development of modern attitudes; and the marginality thesis, discussed in the previous section, has been developed with especial reference to Mexico. However, it is instructive to note in what respects Mexico deviates from the classic pattern of the Third World countries and in what respects it conforms to it. It could be said in general that Mexico conforms most closely to the pattern in its demographic characteristics and least in its political characteristics, and occupies a mixed position with respect to characteristics of its economic and social structure. Thus the Mexican rate of population growth is high; in urbanization, the Mexican experience has been similar to that of the other Latin American countries, and the level of urbanization reached by 1960 (30 percent of the population in cities of 20,000 or more) was close to the Latin American average of 32 percent.[7]

The relative size of Mexican cities, also, resembles the distribution in the developing, rather than in the developed, countries. In the more developed societies, population tends to be distributed among the various cities roughly in accordance with what has been called the "rank-size correlation." The population of the second city tends to be about half that of the largest city, the third city about a third, the fourth about a fourth, and so on. However, in developing countries, or in countries more open to foreign economic influence, the pattern tends rather to be that of the "primate" city; that is, the largest city completely overshadows the rest and is larger than the second city many times over. Thus Mexico City, even without its suburbs, is bigger than the next five cities of the country added together; and the suburbs add over another 50 percent to the population of the capital (see Table 7).

Politically, however, the Mexican pattern is of course distinct from that of the "normal" developing country. This appears most clearly with respect to Germani's eleventh characteristic, the persistence of military intervention; but it is also true that the "archaic patterns in rural areas" that characterize other Third World coun-

Table 7

POPULATION OF MAJOR MEXICAN CITIES AND TOWNS
ACCORDING TO 1970 CENSUS
(PRELIMINARY FIGURES, IN THOUSANDS)

Mexico City metropolitan area	8,541
Guadalajara metropolitan area	1,487
Monterrey metropolitan area	1,177
Puebla	522
León	454
Ciudad Juárez	436
Mexicali	390
Chihuahua	364
Culiacán	359
Tijuana	335
San Luis Potosí	274
Torreón	257
Mérida	254

Source: *Quarterly Economic Review of Mexico, Annual Supplement,* 1970, p. 2.

tries, although they exist in Mexico, are much less part of Mexican reality because of the agrarian reform that has taken place. It is also true that the extent to which modern consumption patterns are restrained by an archaic production system is less in Mexico, as it steadily industrializes, than elsewhere in the Third World.

The whole question of the "asynchronous" character of development alluded to by Germani at several points must also be understood in a rather different sense in Mexico. At first glance it seems especially true of Mexico that political and social mobilization arrived earlier and proceeded at a faster rate than in the classic European pattern, Germani's tenth point. But this refers primarily to the arrival of the initial stages of such mobilization; in Mexico, the complete realization of those processes seems to be taking a markedly longer time than elsewhere in the Third World, as was indicated in the first three chapters of the present book. Mexico has been developing politically for a long time, but still has a long way to go. This can be seen if one compares the figures on voting participation in Mexico and other Latin American countries, a key index to the whole mobilization process.

Mexico stands at precisely the middle of the range of Latin American countries shown in Table 8, with about half of those of voting age actually voting, while the distribution seems to show two fairly clear "modes," the politically more participant countries clustering around the 70-percent mark, the less participant around 33 percent. The evolution of voting participation in Mexico is shown in Table 9.

Table 8

VOTES CAST AS PERCENTAGE OF POPULATION OF VOTING AGE, 1957-68

Country	Percentage Voting	Year
Venezuela	77.7	1968
Bolivia	70.8	1964
Nicaragua	70.7	1963
Argentina	70.1	1963
Dominican Republic	69.8	1966
Costa Rica	67.5	1966
Panama	66.1	1964
Chile	64.5	1964
Uruguay	59.2	1962
MEXICO	52.0	1958
Haiti	48.8	1957
Honduras	43.5	1957
Paraguay	36.3	1958
Brazil	34.2	1960
Peru	33.6	1963
Colombia	33.5	1962
El Salvador	30.8	1962
Ecuador	29.5	1960
Guatemala	18.4	1966

Source: *América en Cifras 1967*, Washington, D.C.: Pan American Union, 1969, p. 5. (Cuba omitted in the original.)

Table 9

ELECTORAL TURNOUT IN POST-REVOLUTIONARY MEXICO, 1911-70

Year	Votes Cast	Total Population	Percentage of Total Population Voting
1911	20,145	15,160,369	0.13
1917	812,928	15,525,000	5.3
1920	1,181,550	14,334,000	8.3
1924	1,593,257	15,240,000	10.4
1928	1,670,453	16,130,000	10.3
1929	2,082,106	16,350,000	12.8
1934	2,265,971	17,776,000	12.8
1940	2,637,582	19,763,000	13.3
1946	2,293,547	22,779,000	10.1
1952	3,651,201	27,415,000	13.3
1958	7,483,403	33,704,000	22.2
1964	9,433,619	41,253,000	22.8
1970	14,027,816	50,718,000	27.6

Sources: (1) Votes Cast:

    (a) 1911-58, Pablo González Casanova, *La democracia en México*, pp. 167-68.

    (b) 1964, *Hispanic American Report*, vol. XVII, no. 8, October 1964, p. 688.

    (c) 1970, *Latin American Digest*, vol. 5, no. 1, October 1970, p. 1.

(2) Population:

    (a) 1911 and 1920, *Anuario Estadistico de los Estados Unidos Mexicanos* (1942); the figures used are actually those given for 1910 and 1921, the closest years available.

    (b) 1917, 1924, and 1928, author's estimates based on data for other years given in *ibid.* and in the *Interamerican Statistical Yearbook 1942*, New York: Macmillan, 1942.

    (c) 1934, 1940, 1946, United Nations *Demographic Yearbook*, 1948.

    (d) 1952, *ibid.*, 1965.

    (e) 1958 and 1964, *ibid.*, 1967.

    (f) 1970, *Datos Básicos de Población en América Latina*, Washington, D.C.: Pan American Union, 1970.

Note: Prior to 1917, presidential elections were indirect; in 1958, women voted for the first time in national elections; in 1970, the voting age was lowered to eighteen.

What all of this means, in effect, is that Germani's ninth point in his catalog of the characteristics of Third World countries—simultaneity rather than sequentiality in modernization processes—needs to be reinterpreted to fit the Mexican case. To be sure, the sequence of the various processes that collectively constitute modernization has not been the same in Mexico as it was in the "classic" case of Western Europe. Nevertheless, these processes are not really occurring simultaneously but have had a sequence of their own in the Mexican context. This could be described as follows:

1. The shift in political control from a traditional landowning oligarchy to the middle class.

2. The *generalized* political mobilization of the stable working class in the major population centers.

3. The *limited* mobilization of the more accessible rural and provincial populations for action in extreme situations, such as civil war and insurrection, only.

4. The beginning of industrialization.

5. The social (not political) mobilization of the masses in the more accessible provincial rural areas.

6. Rapid urbanization.

The total economic, social, and political integration of the *peripheral* masses, those without stable jobs and urban residence, is a long way off, and further stages of development will precede it. That is of course the point of talking about marginal and regional disequilibria, and it signifies that although many problems "hit" simultaneously, nevertheless sequences are involved and have a certain logic, even though these sequences are different from those we are familiar with from Western Europe.

Thus Mexico does not conform altogether to the model that Germani, later in his book, develops of Latin American societies in the stage of mass social mobilization.[8] So far, at least, Mexico has not been characterized by economic stagnation or inflation; attempts at social reform have been successful rather than failures;

and of course military intervention has not been a factor—all of which set Mexico apart from the Latin American norms attributed by Germani to countries in this stage, even though it shares with them such traits as industrialization on the basis of import substitution and unionization under government auspices.

Two causes seem to the present author to bear responsibility for this deviation of Mexico from general Latin American patterns. The first is of course the Mexican Revolution, which broke the social, economic, and political position of the old oligarchy, eliminating the basis for opposition to reform, and constructed the counterpoise, in labor and peasant organization, that was eventually to eliminate military intervention. But the second may be the very marginality of Mexico's peripheral Indian population.

In the Latin American societies that lack a large Indian component—those of predominantly European- or African-descended populations—the absence of the linguistic and cultural gulf separating "national" and "indigenous" sectors of the society means more rapid transmitting of new norms and practices, and more rapid mobilization of the lower social classes.[9] The greater length of time it is taking for the complete social integration of the Mexican masses, that is, the especial persistence of the phenomenon of "marginality" in the Mexican case, derives from the width of the gap between those living by "Indian" and "modern" norms. At the same time it should be noted that it is precisely the slowness of the mobilization process that has saved Mexico from the difficult situation of complete "simultaneity" in the processes of modernization, and has made it possible for the modernization of the economy to take place over the last forty years within a framework of political stability. Where political mobilization is swift, the demand of the aroused masses for economic improvement makes it more likely that governments will follow short-run high-consumption policies rather than the high-investment policies necessary for economic growth. And it is more likely that political turmoil will reign, as governments fall because the rate of economic growth cannot keep pace with the rise in mass demands.

III

A common theme in writings on social development is the polarity between traditionalism and modernism, a polarity not only of societies and institutions,[10] but more especially one of attitudes and views of the world. Characteristic of the "traditional" world view are superstition, resignation in the face of adversity, acceptance of the domination of others, resistance to change. In the modern world-view, the processes that move the world are not mysterious or hostile, but are regular and knowable. It is therefore possible for the rational individual to exert some control over what happens and thus to improve his circumstances. The mutually opposing pairs of characteristics of the two world-views are thus superstition versus rationality, helplessness versus competence, fatalism versus optimism.

From this perspective, although modernization of course implies change in social institutions and structures, it means primarily change in values. Yet it is clear that the opposition between traditional and modern values is not simply the contrast between earlier and later ways of looking at things. In the range of value complexes embodied in different cultures, it is clear that some cultures are *inherently* more "modern" than others in the sense of embodying to a greater extent the values of the "modernism" complex. Alex Inkeles has made this point with respect to the Maya, who he says were more modern in their attitudes to such things as time than the Spaniards who conquered them and whose civilization replaced theirs.[11]

If this is true, if some cultures are *inherently* less "modern" than others, this seems especially to be the case of the cultures of Hispanic America, and that of Mexico in particular. Fatalism in the face of a hostile world and an indifference toward such modern ideas as punctuality are often-cited characteristics of the Mexican masses. Unmodern attitudes seem also marked with respect to politics. As was noted in a previous chapter, attitudes to politics are pervaded by cynicism, the expectation of corruption, the expectation that power will be wielded in an arbitrary and self-interested way, and so on. In the Almond and Verba survey of five countries, Mexican respondents were less likely to expect equal treatment from the police than those in any other country. Fifty-seven percent of those interviewed did not expect to be treated by the police "as well as anyone else," compared with 10 percent in Italy and even fewer in the other countries. Fifty percent of the Mexican respondents did not expect equal treatment by the bureaucracy, compared with 7 percent for the United Kingdom, 9 percent each for Germany and the United States, and 13 percent for Italy.[12] It should be noted that these expectations are not simply arbitrarily induced by the culture, but reflect also experience with the actual behavior of bureaucracy and police; since the latter act in accordance with their culturally determined conceptions of their roles, however, the problem of culture-borne expectations remains.

Those who regard the development process as not necessarily inevitable stress such cultural factors, regarding them as obstacles in the path of development. But will the material changes taking place in Mexico not bring changes in values in their train? Will development change national values, or will national values obstruct development?

Perhaps a preliminary solution to the problem can be suggested along the following lines. A set of attitudes, or a given cultural complex, is determined by several different types of influence. To some extent the complex reflects a given state of material development, its technology and its forms of economic organization. As the material conditions of the society alter as it undergoes economic development, there will clearly be some change in the total culture.

A second determinant of attitudes and values is the social class in which people find themselves. Sociologists have always stressed this, of course, and Oscar Lewis has brought it to the attention of anthropologists, traditionally inclined to lay more emphasis on the cultures of whole societies instead of the subcultures of specific classes, by pointing out the existence of what he has called a culture of poverty; the fact of poverty itself dictates a range of attitudes and behaviors that one encounters in the same social stratum in societies that are otherwise highly different from each other. Thus if one writes about the values of a particular national society, it may be that one is describing not a *national* value complex but a set of values deriving from a particular configuration of social classes.

Nevertheless a third, more strictly national, component of a national value complex still remains after the effects due to these influences have been subtracted. Britain, Germany, and Japan are societies at about the same level of industrial development with rather similar class structures. Yet it is perfectly clear that Englishmen, Germans, and Japanese do not think and behave the same.

In other words, Mexican culture will not prevent development. But though in many ways Mexico will modernize, in many ways it will refuse to become modern; much will remain the same, though not always what ought to remain the same; and for all the influence exerted by the social practices and business methods and political ideals of the "developed" societies, for better or worse the new Mexico that is in process of creation will still remain distinctively Mexican.

IV. IN CONCLUSION

C H A P T E R   T E N

THE MEANING OF
REVOLUTIONARY MEXICO
FOR THE DEVELOPING WORLD

Since the decolonization movement that followed the end of the Second World War, it has become clear that there are certain political problems characteristic not of all countries, nor of certain areas of the world, but of countries in certain stages of political development, on whatever continent they may be located. Thus it has become increasingly clear that the distinctive features of Latin American politics are not merely due to historical and cultural factors peculiar to the Latin American countries themselves, but are to a large extent shared by other countries in similar stages of national development. The Mexican "democratic single party" was long regarded as an isolated case, existing for peculiar reasons of national history, whereas it has since become clear that the single party is instead a characteristic phenomenon of the early stages of national political development, with the Mexican Revolution of 1910 performing a function in the developmental process analogous to the securing of national independence for the African and Asian states.

In many respects, then, an examination of the Mexican experience can prove, because of its priority in time, to be of value in the understanding of the political problems being faced by the newly independent African and Asian countries; the writer has in fact found very great interest in the Mexican system on the part of younger African leaders.

Western political commentators have not been of much help to the Africans here. They have either criticized the new African states for not following in every respect the political etiquette of Britain or the United States, or else excused everything done by African leaders on the grounds that their problems are so great and so different from those of developed Western countries that the norms of Western political behavior do not apply. Africans themselves, seeing that so much in Western politics is inapplicable and so much Western advice unhelpful, have tended to argue that foreign experience is not relevant to their circumstances.

Yet foreign experience *is* relevant to African circumstances—that is, some of it is—while making one's own mistakes is costly, sometimes far too costly. Learning from the experience of others—where it is relevant—is always to be preferred. As it happens, much of Mexico's experience is indeed relevant to the circumstances in which newly independent states of Africa and Asia find themselves.

Although rival conceptions of political development are being used by different students of the problem, a certain area of consensus exists, which may be summarized as follows. In the present era, at least, political development can be regarded as having two aspects, which we can call the quantitative and the qualitative. "Quantitative" political development has as its distinctive characteristic the increase in the proportion of the population that participates, in some sense, in political life. Advances in political development in this sense may come about through revolutionary shifts in the political system; but without such direct political changes, they can also follow more gradually on secular economic and social trends to which Karl Deutsch has given the collective name of "social mobilization"[1]: greater literacy, the expansion of communications, urbanization, and other changes leading to the assumption of national rather than parochial attitudes.

In the "qualitative" sense, political development can be regarded as the increasing tendency for government to function in accordance with its own formal norms; that is, for administrative and judicial organs to administer the law fairly and equitably, for public officials to be honest and competent, for elections to be fairly conducted, for governments to succeed each other in office in the manner prescribed by the country's constitution, for military officers to subordinate themselves to the decisions of their civilian superiors, and so on.[2]

The relations between political development and economic development, and indeed between the quantitative and qualitative aspects of political development itself, are still in the process of elucidation[3] but it is at least clear that political development is not a process that proceeds smoothly without disruption, stagnation, or setbacks. With this in mind, let us examine the key features of Mexico's experience in political development as these compare with experience in the more recently developing African and Asian states.

1. The dominance of the political system by a single party, a central feature of the Mexican polity, has become a typical characteristic of developing countries. It should not be thought that this position of dominance is always the result of the suppression of other parties; many factors make for single-party dominance, even where complete political freedom exists. It is only too common that opposition is prohibited outright or discouraged in various ways, but even where it is not the dominant party may still exercise an overwhelming attraction for voters for reasons varying from its identification with the heroes and symbols of the struggle for independence to its control over patronage appointments and graft. Single-party dominance is generally justified by its apologists as a

necessary restraint on the generalized conflict that would ensue in its absence, leaders in the African countries stressing especially the divisive potentialities of tribalism, and the likelihood that any political conflict would be fought by violent, rather than electoral and parliamentary, means.

In the Mexican case, the dominant party, now called the *Partido Revolucionario Institucional* or PRI, clearly owes its origin to the desire to avoid the armed conflict between various groups that was characteristic of the period before its founding in 1928. The Mexican party has certainly been successful in its mission of containing armed conflict, and the uprisings and civil wars that characterized the period before the founding of the party no longer occur, although of course the party cannot take all of the credit for this situation.

Several distinctive characteristics of the dominant Revolutionary Party in Mexico should be noted. In the first place, it began as a coalition of various Revolutionary organizations, and has always emphasized its inclusive character—thus the PRI goes out of its way to form interest associations of those hitherto unorganized, which are then affiliated with the party. This stands in sharp contrast with the practice of dominant parties elsewhere, which often attempt to maintain an exclusive character, becoming an elite that monopolizes power and its perquisites. Clearly, the Mexican situation is the more healthy one, since it removes the possibility of illegal opposition by disgruntled elements deliberately excluded from positions of power and influence. The mechanism by means of which this expansive and inclusive character is given to the PRI is the party's organization into sectors that compete with each other for members. The competition thus introduced among elements of the party in part supplies the lack of effective competition among parties, for example in performing functions such as interest representation. These sectors are at present designated as labor, agrarian, and popular, the last a catchall for assorted elements supposedly of a bourgeois and petit-bourgeois character. The practice of allowing the sector with the most party members in a specific locality to nominate the party's legislative candidate for that locality, plus the fact that the prestige and authority of a leader depend partly on the number of people he claims to speak for, has encouraged membership drives that contribute to the inclusive character of the party and thus help to maintain its overall strength in the society.

2. The second distinguishing feature of the Mexican political system is the existence of a tolerated opposition. This does not mean that any and all kinds of opposition are tolerated, for some types are regarded as subversive and are illegal; but the limits within which opposition is permitted are usually quite broad, in some respects broader than those that apply in the United States, although the line between the tolerated and the subversive is drawn differently in the two countries. Moreover, the parliamentary opposition is not only tolerated but in some ways encouraged, for example by the amendment to the constitution which introduced a proportional representation feature guaranteeing opposition representation in the Chamber of Deputies.

This toleration of opposition in the Mexican case has important lessons for Africa and Asia. The first of these is that a dominant single party *needs* a critical opposition precisely because its hold on power makes it more liable to err in the direction of abuse of power, the construction of grandiose but impracticable schemes, and so on. A critical opposition can thus strengthen the system rather than weaken it. At the same time, the Mexican case has shown that the elements of strength possessed by a governing revolutionary party, such as its identification with patriotic symbolism, the support given it by those who hope for government jobs, loans, and so forth, and the greater exposure its leaders necessarily receive in the news media, give the party such a substantial edge over its rivals for popular support that its chances of being

defeated by the opposition in a free election are in reality neg-
ligible so long as it does its job well. In other words, a revolutionary
government party *can afford* to tolerate opposition without having
to fear the loss of what it has achieved.

3. However, one must acknowledge that there are several advantages which the dominant party in Mexico enjoys over parties in
most of the newer African and Asian states that enable it to face
opposition with greater equanimity. Post-revolutionary Mexico
has not been confronted, as are many of the African states especially, with hostilities among the population based on linguistic,
tribal, and religious lines. The linguistic and tribal hostilities
which did exist before the arrival of the Spaniards have lost their
divisive power over the 400 years that have passed since the Conquest. The independent African states are less well situated in this
respect because of the much shorter period that elapsed between
the time of European conquest and independence and the fact
that the Europeans did not mingle with the indigenous population
to the extent they did in Latin America; that is, the period of
European rule was not long enough, nor did it go deep enough, to
substitute new alignments based on new forms of political consciousness for the preexisting ones.

4. But even where tribal and other particularistic identifications
are not of significance, there are other reasons why a dominant
revolutionary party may lack overwhelming popular support. One
must remember that societies in their earlier phases of political
development are predominantly societies of peasants. This means
in particular that an innovating elite, regardless of its social and
economic programs, may still lose popular support over religious
questions. Typically, the peasant majority is devout, while the
innovating elite is at least anti-clerical, regarding traditional religious beliefs and practices as impediments to the modernization
of the country. The weak position in which the modernizing elite
is placed by this circumstance when it attempts to institute demo-

cratic political practices is clearly demonstrated by the experience of Turkey, where free elections have led to the removal from power of the modernizing leadership of the Republican Party by an opposition basing itself on the traditional religious feelings of the peasantry. Mexican governments of the 1920s also made the mistake of pursuing anti-clerical policies, which led to violence so extensive that in some areas it took on the character of civil war (the so-called "Cristero Rebellion"). Fortunately for the evolution of the Mexican political system, the leadership realized its error and abandoned its anti-clericalism, negotiating a rapprochement with the Church and developing a system in which the Church can perform its functions without restriction, even though the bulk of the anti-clerical legislation remains, unenforced, on the statute books.

Subsequently, a wide program of land distribution was instituted, effectively tying the peasantry into the Revolutionary Party through their desire to receive land in future distributions, technical help, loans from the government's credit facilities, and so on. Accordingly it has been possible to organize the recipients of land under the reform program as a sector of the official party. This has converted much of the peasantry from a reservoir of potential opposition to one of usually dependable support for government policies.

5. In a manner parallel to its approach to the peasantry, the Revolutionary Party has also succeeded in tying into the system the organized segments of the urban masses through a generally pro-labor policy, coupled with the integration of labor organizations into the governing party. The general loyalty of the key elements of the labor and agrarian sectors has been one of the factors which enabled Revolutionary governments to withstand challenges to their authority by disgruntled military elements in earlier years; agrarian and labor support has in turn been made easier to secure by the fact that the Mexican economy has been steadily expanding.

We come then to a closer examination of the economic and military situations.

6. By a process of trial and error which led in the 1930s, under Cárdenas, to a swing to the left and a policy of economic nationalism and in the 1940s, under Alemán, to a swing to the right and a lack of concern with questions of social justice, Mexico has arrived at a pragmatic policy of the economic "middle way" that combines encouragement for the private sector with initiative in the expansion of the public sector, favorable conditions for foreign investment with the retention of key powers of economic decision in national hands, and augmented benefits for labor with maintenance of a favorable business climate. This non-doctrinaire approach to questions of economic policy has made possible a relatively high rate of overall growth over the long term, without either the abdication of the government's responsibility for setting the general guidelines for national economic development or the complete sacrifice of current consumption in the interest of future growth. While this "mixed" policy has enabled the government to extract the maximum political benefit from the economy at the same time as economic benefits were being produced, this is clearly not a policy which developing countries can arrive at easily. As was noted, Mexico herself developed this type of policy after a period of experimentation which became translated into improvement in policy making only because of the continuity given to government by the existence of the single-party system. In other words, a cumulative learning process was involved. A compromise of this type is of course especially difficult for new states to achieve, it being much more likely that they will straightforwardly choose either a policy of economic nationalism that carries with it a low level of growth, or even stagnation, or else an encouragement of foreign investment that leaves intact the "colonial" structure of the economy and takes out of national hands the power to set the direction of the country's economic development.

7. The Mexican army has been on the whole professionalized and politically neutralized, in the sense that military leaders do not intervene in politics to contest government decisions except perhaps in internal military questions. This is of course a major desideratum of new states, since in a situation in which new institutions lack legitimacy there is an inevitable tendency to resort to force, which leads to the army's necessarily having the last word— a stage through which perhaps most of the independent countries of Africa are now passing. It would not be correct to say that in Mexico the army is completely non-political; the military are used as an instrument of national politics, especially in maintaining order—that is, in putting down organized violent opposition—at the state level; but military involvement in politics no longer takes the form of the attempt to overthrow elected governments, as was typically the case during the 1920s, or even of the attempt to dictate or veto policy on non-military questions.

This change was brought about by a combination of factors. One of these was the professionalization of the military in the sense of the improvement of training, promotion on the basis of merit, the geographic rotation of commands, and so on, as military historians have pointed out.[4] But other, more political, factors were also in play. The steady expansion of the economy, and with it the national budget, made it possible for the appropriation for the military services to increase each year and yet become a smaller and smaller *proportion* of the budget. The sheer passage of time also played a role, as death and old age claimed the individualistic politically minded generals of the Revolutionary era. And it is clear that many military leaders became reconciled to the system as they were given important administrative and party positions, or as they were able to use their official connections to launch highly profitable business enterprises. Nevertheless, the major discouragement to armed revolts was the clear demonstration during the 1920s that revolts could no longer be successful when the government was supported by the mass organizations of labor and peasants. In other words, the regime's immunity from military insurrection was secured by loyalties deriving from its social policy.

8. At this point one should also note the political functions that have been performed in Mexico by the corrupt practices which were so major a feature of the scene in the early post-Revolutionary years and which still persist, although on a smaller scale. It can be said in general that in the early years the payment of bribes and the allowing of leading figures to engage in various forms of profit-making activity were consciously used by the country's leaders to reduce opposition from local military chiefs; President Obregón spoke of the "cannonballs" of fifty thousand pesos he used against rebellious generals. It is clear that bribery has also been used elsewhere to help create parliamentary support for governments attempting to operate new types of political systems, for example by Lord North and his American contemporary Alexander Hamilton. It is only to be expected that a high level of corruption will obtain, similarly, in the new nations of Africa and Asia, partly as a result of the fact that the new political institutions have not yet acquired legitimacy, but also perhaps in part because bribery may deliberately be used by political leaders to acquire support from potential opposition elements.[5] The problem then becomes that of the reduction and elimination of habits of corruption as the functional necessity for them no longer exists. In Mexico the magnitude of corruption in public life has been reduced somewhat in recent years partly as a result of improvements in education, civil service salaries, and business opportunities in the private sector of the economy, but especially because of the firm stand taken, and the better example provided, by the most recent occupants of the presidency.

9. Especially significant in the light of the tendency to perpetuate themselves in office manifested by some African leaders is the distinctive Mexican answer to the problem of succession. One of

the most fundamental of Revolutionary principles has been the doctrine of "no reelection." In keeping with this principle, a Mexican president can today never again be elected to the office after finishing his six-year term. Yet paradoxically the no-reelection provision has been a crucial factor in ensuring the continuity of the Revolutionary regime in Mexico. This is so precisely because the perpetual reelection of a president increases enormously the likelihood that power will be abused, that policy errors and the placing of personal above public interests will go undetected, and that the character and perceptiveness of the power holders will change for the worse over time. The example of Kwame Nkrumah is very much to the point here. At the same time, the perpetuation of the same group of people at the top of the political ladder means that the career aspirations of those lower down are perpetually frustrated, which creates a very dangerous source of disaffection. It was precisely this frustration of career expectations which played a major part in the decision to begin the original Revolution of 1910 against Porfirio Díaz, whose leading collaborators had monopolized the major positions for a quarter of a century at the time the Revolutionary movement began. In Mexico under the no-reelection rule, on the other hand, rewards in the form of advancement to higher positions are guaranteed to those who render competent service. Moreover, this guarantee is the more effective since there is no prospect that the ruling party itself will be turned out of power by a presidential election. The system has in fact created a very able corps of top-level politicians and administrators.

As far as the president himself is concerned, the no-reelection rule can be regarded as a mandate for statesmanship. The president has attained the height of political ambition. He need not, and indeed cannot, worry about tailoring his policies to ensure his reelection. He knows that after six years the records of his administration will by open to scrutiny by other eyes. He can count on appointment to an honorific but well-paying post after his term

is over, and so has no need to worry about the state of his personal
finances. Of couse there is not nor can there be any guarantee of
the quality of his performance in office; but at least many of the
factors which lead to presidents' elsewhere having other concerns
on their minds besides disinterested public service have for the
president of Mexico been removed.

10. One more aspect of the Mexican situation with general significance should be noted. This is the complexity of the causal relations between economic development and political development.
In most of the developing countries of the world, economic and
social development, generated by autonomous factors in the local
and world economies, are leading to the integration of an increasingly greater proportion of the population into national systems
of communication, which in turn leads to a higher level of ("quantitative") political development, conceived of as participation in
politics. This set of relationships is in effect in Mexico too and all
the tendencies are present referred to by Deutsch as components
of the process of "social mobilization." But it should also be noted
that much of the economic development and social mobilization
that has been taking place has occurred as a result of direct and
deliberate government action. Thus, for example, very substantial
government efforts have been made to provide schooling at least
at the elementary level for all Mexican children, efforts have been
made to end the isolation of Indian villages and bring them into
the national community, efforts have been made to organize the
masses and affiliate them with the ruling party, and so on. But the
decision to pursue these policies was implicit in the Revolution
itself. That is, in the Mexican case political change led to economic
and social change, although the latter subsequently reinforced the
former. It should also be added that in Mexico widespread participation in the combat of the early years of the Revolution was
itself a major mobilizing factor quite apart from any economic
and social changes that subsequently came about. In other words,

the Mexican example demonstrates that it is perfectly possible for political development to *precede* economic and social development, even though the causal relation appears usually to be in the opposite direction.[6]

Of course Mexico's social, economic, demographic, and political characteristics are her own and it is not to be expected that the specific problems faced by other developing countries will resemble in detail those which Mexico has met and in part solved. Yet it is also clear that the lessons of Mexico's development can be learned with profit, for her achievements—a high rate of economic growth, the capacity to combine foreign investment with national control, political continuity coexisting with a tolerated opposition and a high order of civil liberties—represent in general the goals of other developing countries, while to reach them Mexico has had to surmount traditions of foreign influence, political violence, authoritarianism, and military intervention, which are likely to be shared by other countries undergoing development. The path followed was the expensive one of trial and error, expensive in terms of human lives and suffering. But one may hope that the Mexican demonstration of how the goals of developing countries can be reached may make it possible for other countries in similar situations to achieve what Mexico has accomplished, but at a lower cost in human values.

APPENDIX

At present the formal structure of the official party is based firmly on its division into three sectors. At the national level, thus, the party statutes[1] provide that the supreme legislative body of the party is the National Assembly, which is supposed to meet normally every six years, although it may be summoned into special session. The number of delegates to the National Assembly is on the order of a thousand; the three sectors are represented equally. Between sessions of the National Assembly, supervision of the real directive organ of the party, the National Executive Committee (CEN), is supposed to be exercised by the National Council, a body representative of the state and sector organizations, which takes its decisions by ballots in which each sector has one vote. The CEN consists of a president, a secretary-general, and a staff director (*Oficial Mayor*), secretaries representing each of the three sectors, one "secretary of political action" representing the party's members in each of the houses of the national legislature, chosen by the party caucuses in each house, and the party secretaries of organization, press and propaganda, and finance.

This set of relationships rather resembles the formal organizational structure of the Communist Party of the Soviet Union, in which, similarly, the party secretariat is supervised by the party presidium, which is responsible to the party congress. However, as in the CPSU, while the formal lines of control and election run in one direction, the actual power relations run very much the other way. That is, the president and secretary-general of. the national party are very much the men of the president of the republic, and they have the last word in all party matters.

State Executive Committees exist in the thirty-two "federal entities" of the republic (that is, in the twenty-nine states, the two territories, and the Federal District). Their composition is an abbreviated version of that of the National Executive Committee and for all intents and purposes they are the creatures of the state, territorial, or district governor. The president and secretary-general of the state committee are elected by the state assemblies just as the president and secretary-general of the national party are elected by the National Assembly, but, needless to say, this "election" is of the nature of a ratification of a decision already made. At the local level, "municipal" committees each of five members are supposed to exist for each county in Mexico, and for each election district in the federal capital and the federal territories. Although parity for the three sectors of the party is not stipulated for the municipal level, the municipal committee, which is formally elected by the municipal assembly, is to have added to it representatives of any of the sectors which have organizations in the *municipio*. Precinct committees, which choose representatives to the municipal assemblies, are elected by an assembly of all party members in the precinct.[2]

NOTES

PREFACE

1. *American Political Science Review,* vol. 51, no. 4, December 1957.
2. New York: Harper and Row, 1957.
3. Eventually published as "The Theory of the Weimar Presidency," *The Review of Politics,* vol. 21, no. 4, October 1959.
4. "The Political Development of Mexico," *American Political Science Review,* vol. 55, no. 2, June 1961; "Hitler's Anti-Semitism: a Political Appraisal," *Public Opinion Quarterly,* vol. 24, no. 4, autumn 1961; "On the Dangers of Copying from the British," *Political Science Quarterly,* vol. 57, no. 3, September 1962.

CHAPTER ONE

1. See the account of this conference in Froylán C. Manjárrez, *La Jornada Institucional,* México, D.F.: Talleres Gráficos, 1930, vol. I, p. 68.
2. See Virginia Prewitt, *Reportage on Mexico,* New York: E. P. Dutton, 1941, chapter 11; James W. Wilkie, *The Mexican Revolution: Federal Expenditure and Social Change Since 1910,* Berkeley and Los Angeles: University of California Press, 1967, p. 180, for the opinion of Marte R. Gómez; Frank R. Brandenburg, *The Making of Modern Mexico,* Englewood Cliffs, N.J.: Prentice-Hall, 1964, p. 93.
3. *The Seizure of Political Power,* New York: Philosophical Library, 1958, p. 51.
4. *Terror and Progress, USSR,* Cambridge, Mass.: Harvard University Press, 1954, p. 31.
5. A good account of the organization of the PRI is in Leon Vincent Padgett's unpublished Ph.D. dissertation, *Popular Participation in the Mexican "One-Party" System,* Northwestern University, 1955. Party struc-

ture is also discussed in Robert E. Scott's *Mexican Government in Transition,* Urbana: University of Illinois Press, 1959.

6. The potential of labor, it should be noted, lay in its role in urban violence more than in pitched battles, although "labor battalions" did participate in some military campaigns.

7. There is an interesting British precedent here. One school of thought has it that Edward I began to summon burghers and knights to the House of Commons after he appreciated their fighting potential as a result of their participation against him in the Battle of Evesham. See Isaac Kramnick, "Augustan Politics and English Historiography: The Debate on the English Past, 1730-35," *History and Theory,* vol. VI, no. 1, 1967, p. 36.

8. On the importance of armed peasants in defeating the revolt, see the comments of Jesús Silva Herzog in James Wilkie and Edna Monzón de Wilkie, *México visto en el siglo XX: entrevistas de historia oral,* México: Instituto Mexicano de Investigaciones Económicas, 1969, p. 637. It should be noted that labor union members fought for the rebel side also in 1923. See Edwin Lieuwen, *Mexican Militarism,* Albuquerque: University of New Mexico Press, 1968, p. 73.

9. This is also the conclusion of former President Portes Gil, who organized the party's agrarian sector. See Emilio Portes Gil, *La crisis política de la revolución y la próxima elección presidencial,* Mexico, D.F.: Ediciones Botas, 1957, p. 20. Portes Gil describes how he relied on the armed peasantry of Hidalgo, San Luís Potosí, and Tamaulipas in a critical situation during his own presidency, in Wilkie and Wilkie, *op. cit.,* p. 513.

10. *Zapata and the Mexican Revolution,* New York: Knopf, 1969, p. 374.

11. Obregón to Frank Bohn, February 12, 1924, quoted in Randall Hansis, "Alvaro Obregón, the Mexican Revolution, and the Politics of Consolidation, 1920-1924," unpublished Ph.D. dissertation, University of New Mexico, 1970, p. 224.

12. *The Role of the Chief Executive in Mexico,* unpublished Ph.D. dissertation, University of California at Berkeley, 1947, p. 476. Still today, army officers are allowed time off with pay to engage in income-producing activities. According to one estimate, the average officer earns an amount equal to 40 percent of his regular salary in "outside" activities. This is legitimate work, and not graft, however. Franklin D. Margiotta, *The Mexican Military: A Case Study in Nonintervention,* unpublished M.A. thesis, Georgetown University, June 1968, pp. 84-85.

13. Bertram Wolfe and Diego Rivera, *Portrait of Mexico,* New York: Covici, Friede, 1937, p. 199.

14. A classic discussion of the techniques used in de-emphasizing the

military is Virginia Prewitt, "The Mexican Army Today," *Foreign Affairs*, April 1941. The subject has received its definitive treatment in Edwin Lieuwen's *Mexican Militarism*, Albuquerque: University of New Mexico Press, 1968.

15. For example, Anthony Downs, *An Economic Theory of Democracy*, New York: Harper and Row, 1957; or E. E. Schattschneider, *Party Government*, New York: Rinehart, 1942.

CHAPTER TWO

1. See, for example, James W. Wilkie, *The Mexican Revolution: Federal Expenditure and Social Change Since 1910*, Berkeley and Los Angeles: University of California Press, 1967, pp. 180-81; Frank R. Brandenburg, *The Making of Modern Mexico*, Englewood Cliffs, N.J.: Prentice-Hall, 1964, pp. 223-43.

2. *Autobiografía de la revolución mexicana*, México: Instituto Mexicano de Cultura, 1964, pp. 633-34.

3. Marte R. Gómez, cited in Wilkie, *op. cit.*, p. 180. According to Portes Gil, the government candidate, General Avila Camacho, won the election, but with 75 percent of the vote, not the 94 percent announced as the official result. James W. Wilkie and Edna Monzón de Wilkie, *México visto en el siglo XX: entrevistas de historia oral*, Mexico: Instituto Mexicano de Investigaciones Económicas, 1969, p. 598.

4. Portes Gil, *op. cit.*, p. 469.

5. Pablo González Casanova, *La democracia en México*, México: Ediciones Era, 1964, p. 241.

6. William J. Blough, "Party Identification and Political Attitudes in Mexico," mimeographed unpublished paper, University of Houston, April 1968, p. 5.

7. *Ibid.*, p. 7.

8. To the writer's knowledge, none of the many people who have impugned the counting of ballots in Mexico has attempted to make this rather simple comparison with the survey results.

9. In Almond's and Verba's 1959 urban sample, this was 87 percent of PRI identifiers and 70 percent of PAN identifiers, Blough, *op. cit.*, p. 7.

10. Jose Luis Reyna, *Algunos aspectos políticos de México*, Tesis para el título de licenciado en ciencias sociales, Universidad Nacional Autónoma de México, 1967, pp. 77, 111. Reyna's use of a population size of 100,000 to define "urban residence" may have weakened the point. The findings of Barry Ames, which do not show a relationship between degree of development and turnout, seem to be due to an error in the opposite direction. "Bases of Support for Mexico's Dominant Party," *American Political Science Review*, vol. 64, no. 1, March 1970. The use by Ames of a

population size of 2,500 to define "urban residence" makes it impossible to distinguish between small villages and genuine cities.

11. Lester W. Milbrath, *Political Participation: How and Why Do People Get Involved in Politics?* Chicago: Rand McNally, 1965, pp. 97-98, 119.

12. Ames, *op. cit.,* p. 167.

13. González Casanova, *op. cit.,* pp. 106, 239-49.

14. V. O. Key, Jr., *Politics, Parties, and Pressure Groups,* New York: Thomas Y. Crowell, 1958, 4th ed., p. 630; Milbrath, *op. cit.,* p. 96.

15. David E. Butler, "Appendix: Analysis of the Results," in H. G. Nicholas, *The British General Election of 1950,* London: Macmillan, 1951, p. 318.

16. "Electoral Behavior and Political Development in El Salvador," *Journal of Politics,* vol. 31, no. 2, May 1969, p. 417.

17. "Soviet Elections as a Measure of Dissent: The Missing One Percent," *American Political Science Review,* vol. 62, no. 3, September 1968.

18. Reyna, *op. cit.,* p. 101.

19. *Ibid.,* p. 106.   20. *Ibid.,* p. 114.

21. Braulio Maldonado, *Baja California,* 2d ed., México: Costa-Amic, 1960, p. 19.

CHAPTER THREE

1. *Excelsior,* August 12, 1968. Portes Gil's sourer version has it that (between 1946 and 1958) an "undefined and indeterminate group" chose party candidates for office without paying attention to anything or anybody. Emilio Portes Gil, *Autobiografía de la revolución mexicana,* México: Instituto Mexicano de Cultura, 1964, p. 621.

2. *Excelsior,* August 12, 1968.

3. This episode is discussed in Robert K. Furtak, *Revolutionspartei und politische Stabilität in México* [sic], Hamburg: Uebersee-Verlag, 1969, pp. 80-81.

4. See Antonio Ugalde, *Power and Conflict in a Mexican Community: A Study of Political Integration,* Albuquerque: University of New Mexico Press, 1970, pp. 161-66.

5. When Madrazo was killed in a plane crash in 1969, the conspiracy minded even suspected foul play.

CHAPTER FOUR

1. I do not mean to suggest that any one person or set of people "runs" Mexico. The situation is more complex than that, and of course power is shared. This softens the point of the questions asked by Carolyn and Martin Needleman in their interesting critical article "Who Rules Mex-

ico? A Critique of Some Current Views of the Mexican Political Process,"
Journal of Politics, vol. 31, no. 4, November 1969.

2. Frank R. Brandenburg, *The Making of Modern Mexico,* Englewood Cliffs, N.J.: Prentice-Hall, 1964, p. 144.

3. *Ibid.,* pp. 5-7.

4. Pablo González Casanova, *La democracia en México,* México, D.F.: Ediciones Era, 1965, p. 21.

5. Rafael Segovia, "El PRI en la coyuntura política actual," mimeographed unpublished paper, 1968.

6. Rodolfo Stavenhagen, "Un modelo para el estudio de las organizaciones políticas en México," *Revista Mexicana de Sociología,* vol. 29, no. 2 (April-June 1967).

7. Segovia, *op. cit.,* p. 3. Linz's definition is taken from his chapter "An Authoritarian Regime: Spain" in Erik Allardt and Yrjö Littunen, *Cleavages, Ideologies and Party Systems,* Transactions of the Westmarck Society, vol. X, Helsinki: The Academic Bookstore, 1964, p. 297.

8. "Alternative Courses of Political Development," a selection from *Political Development in New States,* reprinted in Jason L. Finkle and Richard W. Gable, *Political Development and Social Change,* New York: Wiley, 1966, pp. 458-77.

9. See the discussion on this point between James Wilkie and Marte R. Gómez in James Wilkie and Edna Monzón de Wilkie, *México visto en el siglo XX: entrevistas de historia oral,* México: Instituto Mexicano de Investigaciones Económicas, 1969, p. 114, *et seq.*

10. "Institutionalized Revolution Drifts to the Right," *Auténtico,* vol. 1, no. 1, August-September, 1969, pp. 5-6.

CHAPTER FIVE

1. Oscar Lewis, "Mexico Since Cárdenas," in Richard N. Adams *et al., Social Change in Latin America Today: Its Implications for United States Policy,* New York: Harper, 1960, pp. 322-29.

2. "Mexico: The Lop-Sided Revolution" in Claudio Veliz, ed., *Obstacles to Change in Latin America,* London and New York: Oxford University Press, 1969.

3. *The Dilemma of Mexico's Development,* Cambridge, Mass.: Harvard University Press, 1963, p. 94.

4. As President Carlos Lleras Restrepo of Colombia and others have pointed out, this capital is most advantageously received in the form of bonds, which are amortized within a fixed period, rather than as stock participation, dividends on which constitute a charge on the economy indefinitely.

5. See for example the opening statements of the "economic policy"

section of Díaz Ordaz's third "State of the Union" message, September 1, 1967.

6. *The Economist* (edición para América Latina), April 5, 1968, p. 13.

7. See Andrew Shonfield, *Modern Capitalism: the Changing Balance of Public and Private Power,* New York: Oxford University Press, 1965, *passim.*

8. The term *prestanombre* has even been coined for Mexicans who "lend their names" in this and other types of arrangements to get around nationalist laws.

9. It was estimated around 1967 that 40 percent of Mexico's workers received less than the minimum wage. Cited in Antonio Ugalde, *Power and Conflict in a Mexican Community: A Study of Political Integration,* Albuquerque: University of New Mexico Press, 1970, p. 58.

10. Folke Dovring, *Land Reform and Productivity: the Mexican Case, Analysis of Census Data,* University of Wisconsin Land Tenure Center (LTC 63), mimeographed, January 1969, p. 22.

11. *Ibid.,* p. 16.   12. *Ibid.,* p. 10.

13. In practice, the legal restrictions on the use of *ejido* land are sometimes ignored; that is, sometimes the land is rented to neighbors, leased to large-scale mechanized farming operations, or informally "sold." For examples, see Moïsés González Navarro, *La confederación nacional campesina: un grupo de presión en la reforma agraria mexicana,* Mexico: Costa-Amic, 1968, pp. 294, 296.

14. Rodolfo Stavenhagen *et al., Neolatifundismo y explotación,* Mexico: Nuestro Tiempo, 1968, p. 19.

15. Dovring, *op. cit.,* p. 4.

16. See Jesús Silva Herzog, *El agrarismo mexicano y la reforma agraria: exposición y crítica,* 2d ed., México, D.F., 1964, p. 372.

17. *Ibid.,* p. 388.

18. This charge is made by Víctor Alba in "Populism and National Awareness in Latin America," occasional publication no. 6 of the Center for Latin American Studies of the University of Kansas, June 1966, p. 17.

19. Rodolfo Stavenhagen, "Marginalidad y participación en la reforma agraria mexicana," *Revista Latinoamericana de Sociología,* vol. 5, no. 2, July 1969, pp. 261, 266.

20. *Ibid.,* pp. 269, 271.

21. Dovring, *op. cit.,* p. 6.

CHAPTER SIX

1. For the most comprehensive study with this orientation, see Edwin Lieuwen, *Mexican Militarism,* Albuquerque: University of New Mexico Press, 1968, especially the Epilogue.

2. *Mexican Government in Transition,* Urbana: University of Illinois Press, 1959, p. 134.

3. Frank Brandenburg, *The Making of Modern Mexico,* Englewood Cliffs, N.J.: Prentice-Hall, 1964, p. 94.

4. See Jorge Alberto Lozoya, *El ejército mexicano (1911-1965),* México: El Colegio de México, 1970, pp. 73-75.

5. See Lozoya, *op. cit.,* p. 85.

6. Alfonso Corona del Rosal, *Moral militar y civismo,* 2d ed., México: Ediciones en Marcha, Estado Mayor Presidencial, 1952.

7. Cited in Lozoya, *op. cit.,* p. 85.

8. See Lozoya, *op. cit.,* pp. 78-82.

9. *Ibid.,* pp. 58-60.

10. Franklin D. Margiotta, *The Mexican Military: A Case Study in Nonintervention,* M.A. thesis, Georgetown University, June 1968, p. 106.

11. *Ibid.,* p. 82.

12. See the data given in Lieuwen, *op. cit.,* p. 153.

13. This point is brought out by Joseph E. Loftus in *Latin American Defense Expenditures, 1938-1965,* Rand Memorandum RM-5310-PR/ISA, January 1968, pp. 15-16, 66.

14. Unfortunately, in the otherwise stimulating work of James R. Wilkie on the Mexican budget the domestic political relationships are obscured by the use of figures corrected for inflation or stated in stable pesos per capita. It seems *a priori* unlikely that budgetary amounts are thought of by political or military figures primarily in those terms. James W. Wilkie, *The Mexican Revolution: Federal Expenditure and Social Change Since 1910,* Berkeley and Los Angeles: University of California Press, 1967, pp. 102-03, 293.

15. See Margiotta, *op. cit.,* pp. 131, 134-35. Tables giving the numbers of military officers holding such posts are provided by Lyle McAlister in McAlister *et al., The Military in Latin American Sociopolitical Evolution: Four Case Studies,* Washington, D.C.: American University Center for Research in Social Systems, 1970, pp. 238-40.

16. McAlister, *op. cit.,* p. 236.

CHAPTER SEVEN

1. Gordon W. Hewes, "Mexicans in Search of the 'Mexican': Notes on Mexican National Character Studies," *American Journal of Economics and Sociology,* January 1954; Michael Maccoby, "On Mexican National Character," *The Annals,* March 1967.

2. For a brilliant statement of the composite picture, see Octavio Paz, *The Labyrinth of Solitude,* translated by Lysander Kemp, New York: Grove Press, 1961.

3. Maccoby found the key characteristics of his villagers to be "fatalism, distrust, and hopelessness." "Love and Authority: A Study of Mexican Villagers," *Atlantic*, vol. 213, no. 3, March 1964.

4. On this point, see Maccoby, "On Mexican National Character," *op. cit.*, pp. 68-69; Santiago Ramírez, *El mexicano: psicología de sus motivaciones*, México, D.F.: Editorial Pax-México, 4th ed., 1966, p. 62; Samuel Ramos, *Profile of Man and Culture in Mexico*, translated by Peter G. Earle, Austin: University of Texas Press, 1962, Chapter III; Aniceto Aramoni, *Psicoanálisis de la dinámica de un pueblo*, México, D.F.: Universidad Nacional Autónoma de México, 1961, p. 271.

5. "Death is a necessary attribute of the hero in Mexico," writes Jorge Carrión in *Mito y magia del mexicano*, México, D.F.: Porrúa y Obregón, 1952, p. 30. "Mexico is a country where only the dead are heroes," says Carlos Fuentes, quoted in Luis Haiss, "Carlos Fuentes: Mexico's Metropolitan Eye," *New Mexico Quarterly*, spring 1966.

6. On the nature of historical facts, see the perceptive remarks of E. H. Carr in Chapter I of *What is History?* New York: Knopf, 1963.

7. For example, his contemporary Theodore Roosevelt, who called Díaz "the greatest statesman of his time."

8. This is confirmed by the observation that the same themes predominate in the modern Mexican novel.

9. Carrión, *op. cit.*, p. 7.

10. The process of externalization is discussed, in its political implications, by M. Brewster Smith, Jerome S. Bruner, and Robert W. White, *Opinions and Personality*, New York: Wiley, 1956, *passim*. Francisco González Pineda also regards the "official" history of Mexico as externalization; see *El mexicano: su dinámica psicosocial*, 3d ed., México, D.F.: Editorial Pax-México, 1966, pp. 22-23, 109-10.

11. On this point Oscar Lewis's *The Children of Sanchez*, New York: Random House, 1961, is very good.

12. Data on this point are reported in José E. Iturriaga, *La estructura social y cultural de México*, México, D.F.: Fondo de Cultura Económica, 1951.

13. Ramírez found that 32 percent of a sample of Federal District households lacked fathers *at the time he took his survey, op. cit.*, pp. 87-88.

14. An average of 2.3 per household in another survey reported by Ramírez, *op. cit.*, p. 95.

15. From a study of student and non-student attitudes in Jalapa, Veracruz: "neither the students, the general populace nor the youths in the latter group place much trust in normal interpersonal relations." William S. Tuohy and Barry Ames, *Mexican Students in Politics: Rebels Without Allies?* Social Science Foundation and Graduate School of International Affairs, University of Denver, monograph series, 1970, p. 9.

16. The best source here is again Oscar Lewis. See *Life in a Mexican Village: Tepotzlán Restudied,* Urbana: University of Illinois Press, 1951.

17. Maccoby, "Love and Authority," p. 124.

18. "They conceive of authority only as an irrational punishing force." Description of boys' games in Michael Maccoby, Nancy Modiano, and Patricia Lander, "Games and Social Character in a Mexican Village," *Psychiatry,* vol. 27, no. 2, May 1964, p. 155.

19. By Gabriel Almond and Sidney Verba, abridged ed., Boston: Little, Brown and Co., 1965.

20. *Ibid.,* pp. 310-12. Needless to say, the writer believes that the authors' explanation for these results, which they give in historical terms, is inadequate.

21. The present writer finds hard to swallow González Pineda's conception of the president as a *mother* figure, *op. cit.,* p. 48.

22. This seems supported by the results of political socialization research in the United States, if one can assume that political attitudes among the less sophisticated remain similar to the attitudes they held as children without undergoing evolution, as do the attitudes of those securing education. Among American children, "Idealization of authority occurs early in life, as political figures are viewed as extraordinarily benign." Richard G. Niemi, in a review of David Easton and Jack Dennis, *Children in the Political System, American Political Science Review,* vol. 64, no. 1, March 1970, p. 190. Niemi goes on, "This halo, of course, wears off as children progress through the elementary grades." But the average Mexican progresses not very far, if at all, through the elementary grades, so perhaps the halo never wears off. In Chapter Two it was mentioned that the population group most loyal to the PRI, by education, consists of those with primary schooling only.

CHAPTER EIGHT

1. Luis Unikel Spector, cited in *The News* (Mexico City) of March 6, 1969.

2. Lawrence A. Alschuler, *Political Participation and Urbanization in Mexico,* Ph.D. dissertation, Northwestern University, 1967, p. 122.

3. Wayne A. Cornelius, Jr., "Urbanization as an Agent in Latin American Political Instability: the Case of Mexico," *American Political Science Review,* September 1969, p. 5.

4. In Mexico, several terms are used; perhaps *colonia proletaria* is most common, although it does not always distinguish clearly between "mushroom" shantytowns and older slum districts.

5. Cornelius, *op. cit.,* p. 7.

6. The evidence on this point is marshalled overwhelmingly by William Mangin in his "Latin American Squatter Settlements: A Problem and A Solution," *Latin American Research Review,* vol. II, no. 3, summer 1967, p. 68.

7. For a discussion of the differences between the urban slum and the shantytown, see Richard W. Patch, "La Parada, Lima's Market, Part III: *Serrano* to *Criollo,* A Study of Assimilation," American Universities Field Staff Reports, March 1967, p. 13; and Lloyd Rogler, "Slum Neighborhoods in Latin America," *Journal of Inter-American Studies,* vol. IX, no. 4, October 1967, p. 514.

8. About 80 percent of lower-class migrants were satisfied with their decision to move to Buenos Aires. Gino Germani, "La ciudad como mecanismo integrador," *Revista Mexicana de Sociología,* vol. 29, no. 3, July-September, 1967, p. 403. According to the 1960 Mexican census, in the Federal District the living conditions of migrants were comparable to those of the urban-born in the availability of municipal services and the ownership of appliances, Cornelius, *op. cit.,* p. 6. Migrants were more hopeful about the economic future of their families than the urban-born, *ibid.,* p. 10. Although the wage levels of migrants were somewhat below those of the urban-born, they were higher than those previously known by migrants from rural areas, *ibid.,* pp. 9-10.

9. At the time of writing, these results had not become available in published form.

10. Cornelius, *op. cit.,* p. 9.

11. *Ibid.,* p. 13.

12. This factor and several related ones are discussed in Daniel Goldrich, "Toward a Comparative Study of Politicization," in Dwight B. Heath and Richard N. Adams, eds., *Contemporary Cultures and Societies of Latin America,* New York: Random House, 1965, pp. 363 *et seq.* After twenty years of urban residence, only 13 percent of Mexican migrants surveyed regularly followed political events and only about half even paid any attention to national election campaigns, which saturate the communications media; Cornelius, *op. cit.,* p. 15.

13. See Goldrich, *op. cit.,* and Richard N. Morse, "Urban Society in Contemporary Latin America," *Ventures,* vol. VII, no. 2, fall 1967.

14. José A. Moreno, *Sociological Aspects of the Dominican Revolution,* Ithaca, N.Y.: Cornell University Latin American Studies Program, dissertation series, June 1967, p. 133.

15. This point has been discussed in Chapter One.

16. Ugalde, *Power and Conflict in a Mexican Community: A Study of Political Integration,* Albuquerque: University of New Mexico Press, 1970, p. 148.

17. See Pablo González Casanova, *La democracia en México*. México: Ediciones Era, 1964, p. 106.

18. Cornelius, *op. cit.*, p. 17.

19. The best discussion of the attitudes appropriate to the developed polity can be found in Gabriel Almond and Sidney Verba, *The Civic Culture*, abridged ed. Boston: Little, Brown and Co., 1965.

20. This is reflected in the finding by Almond and Verba that over half their Mexican sample expected that they would *not* receive equal (i.e., fair) treatment by the bureaucracy and the police. This group was several times as large as the corresponding groups in the other countries surveyed (the United States, Britain, Germany, and Italy), *op. cit.*, p. 70. The authors regard this response as a function of culturally determined attitudes on the part of their Mexican respondents. The present writer would regard this as partly the case but believes it also reflects quite correct perceptions of the factual situation.

21. Michael Maccoby has found in his study of a Mexican village that only a minority (although a large one) show the *machista* syndrome, and only about 30 percent of his respondents could be called authoritarian personalities. Although he goes on to argue that Mexican character structure could support more democratic attitudes if society and government practices changed so as to warrant them, he does not discuss the possibility that authoritarian characteristics may be strengthened by urbanization. "On Mexican National Character," *The Annals,* March 1967.

22. See José E. Iturriaga, *La estructura social y cultural de México,* México, D.F.: Fondo de Cultura Económica, 1951, *passim.*

23. A good example is *Los Problemas Mayores de México y de Nuestro Tiempo,* the platform adopted by the party's national convention in 1961.

24. The story of how the party's evolution took place is told in L. Vincent Padgett, *The Mexican Political System,* Boston: Houghton Mifflin, 1966, pp. 68-73.

CHAPTER NINE

1. This so-called "step migration" seems typical for some countries of Latin America, as it was for nineteenth-century England. See Bruce H. Herrick, *Urban Migration and Economic Development in Chile,* Cambridge, Mass.: M.I.T. Press, 1965, p. 51. In Mexico, however, this effect seems not so great, apparently because of the greater attractive power and accessibility of Mexico City.

2. The two greatest rates of population growth during the 1950-60 decade were shown by the states of Baja California Norte (232 percent), and Tamaulipas (61 percent). Both rates were greater than that for the

Federal District (49 percent), which includes Mexico City. These rates of growth have continued since 1960. Of the total number of people moving their residence during the 1950-60 decade, between a third and a half went to Mexico City and environs and 29 percent went to the five northern border states of Baja California Norte, Sonora, Chihuahua, Coahuila, and Tamaulipas. Kennett Cott, "Trends in Mexican Migration," unpublished paper, University of New Mexico, 1968.

3. Pablo González Casanova, *La democracia en México*, México: Ediciones Era, 1965.

4. For data supporting the latter conclusion, see Oscar Lewis, "Mexico Since Cárdenas," in Richard N. Adams, *et al., Social Change in Latin America Today*, New York: Harper, 1960, pp. 320-26. It should be noted, however, that the maldistribution of income cited by Lewis derived partly from the inflation that was still a factor in the early 1950s. Since the devaluation and stabilization of the peso in 1954, inequality deriving from this effect has been substantially reduced.

5. According to one recent study, disparities in income between regions rise in the early stages of development, but decline and even disappear as the economy matures. Jeffrey G. Williamson, "Regional Inequality and the Process of National Development: A Description of the Patterns," *Economic Development and Cultural Change*, vol. 13, no. 4, Part II, July 1965.

6. Gino Germani, *Sociología de la modernización*, Buenos Aires: Paidos, 1969, pp. 10-11.

7. *Ibid.*, pp. 190-91.

8. *Ibid.*, pp. 56-57.

9. This question is discussed in Chapter Six of my *Political Development in Latin America*, New York: Random House, 1968.

10. Of course, a tremendous range of variation is concealed within the category of "traditional" societies, but we need not deal with this problem in the present context.

11. "The Modernization of Man" in Myron Weiner, ed., *Modernization: the Dynamics of Growth*, New York: Basic Books, 1966, p. 143.

12. Gabriel Almond and Sidney Verba, *The Civic Culture: Political Attitudes and Democracy in Five Nations*, abridged ed., Boston: Little, Brown and Co., 1965, p. 70.

CHAPTER TEN

1. "Social Mobilization and Political Development," *American Political Science Review*, September 1961.

2. For some purposes the alternative formulation the writer has used

previously may be preferable: if one thinks of a continuum of methods of resolving disputes ranging from the use of force through bargaining techniques to administration and law enforcement, a country is more developed "qualitatively" the more it solves its disputes by techniques from the "administration and law enforcement," rather than the "violence" end of the spectrum; see Chapter One.

3. The present writer has found that for the Latin American countries a direct relation exists between economic development and political development, and an inverse relation between the two aspects of political development. See Chapter 5 of his *Political Development in Latin America: Instability, Violence and Evolutionary Change,* New York: Random House, 1968.

4. See Edwin Lieuwen, *Arms and Politics in Latin America,* revised ed., New York: Praeger, 1961, Chapter IV; and, by the same author, *Mexican Militarism,* Albuquerque: University of New Mexico Press, 1968.

5. The functions of bribery in developing countries are discussed by Joseph S. Nye in "Corruption & Political Development: A Cost-Benefit Analysis," *American Political Science Review,* June 1967.

6. It remains true, as recent historical scholarship has demonstrated, that economic development took place under the Díaz administration which helped to create the conditions for the outbreak of the Revolution.

APPENDIX

1. *Declaración de Principios, Programa de Acción, Estatutos,* México: Partido Revolucionario Institucional, 1969, pp. 75-130.

2. Various deviations from the party statutes at the local level are described in Mario Ezcurdia, *Análisis teórico del Partido Revolucionario Institucional,* México: Costa-Amic, 1968, especially Chapter 9.

SELECTED BIBLIOGRAPHY

I. BOOKS

Alba, Víctor. *Las ideas sociales contemporáneas en México*. México: Fondo de Cultura Económica, 1960.

———. *El militarismo: ensayo sobre un fenómeno politicosocial iberoamericano*. México: Instituto de Investigaciones Sociales, Universidad Nacional Autónoma de México, 1959.

Almond, Gabriel, and Sidney Verba. *The Civic Culture: Political Attitudes and Democracy in Five Nations*, abridged ed. Boston: Little, Brown and Co., 1965.

Anguiano Equihua, Roberto. *Las finanzas del sector público en México*. México: Universidad Nacional Autónoma de México, 1968.

Aramoni, Aniceto. *Psicoanálisis de la dinámica de un pueblo*. México, D.F.: Universidad Nacional Autónoma de México, 1961.

Bermúdez, María Elvira. *La vida familiar del mexicano*. México: Antigua Librería Robredo, 1955.

Brandenburg, Frank R. *The Making of Modern Mexico*. Englewood Cliffs, N.J.: Prentice-Hall, 1964.

Castañeda, Jorge. *Mexico and the United Nations*. New York: Carnegie Endowment for International Peace, 1958.

Cline, Howard F. *Mexico: Revolution to Evolution 1940-1960*. New York and London: Oxford University Press, 1962.

———. *The United States and Mexico*, revised ed. New York: Atheneum, 1963.

Corona del Rosal, Alfonso. *Moral militar y civismo*, 2d ed. México: Ediciones en Marcha, Estado Mayor Presidencial, 1952.

Crawford, William Rex. *A Century of Latin American Thought*, revised ed. Cambridge, Mass.: Harvard University Press, 1961.

D'Antonio, William U., and William H. Form. *Influentials in Two Border Cities: a Study in Community Decision-Making*. Notre Dame: University of Notre Dame Press, 1965.

Delhumeau, Antonio, et al. *México: realidad política de sus partidos.* México: Instituto Mexicano de Estudios Políticos, 1970.

Dulles, J. W. F. *Yesterday in Mexico.* Austin: University of Texas Press, 1960.

Ezcurdia, Mario. *Análisis teórico del Partido Revolucionario Institucional.* México, D.F.: Costa-Amic, 1968.

Fuentes Díaz, Vicente. *Los partidos políticos de México.* Mexico: published by author, 1956.

Furtak, Robert K. *Revolutionspartei und politische Stabilität in México* [sic]. Hamburg: Uebersee-Verlag, 1969.

Germani, Gino. *Sociología de la modernización.* Buenos Aires: Paidos, 1969.

Glade, William P., and Charles W. Anderson. *The Political Economy of Mexico.* Madison: University of Wisconsin Press, 1963.

González Casanova, Pablo. *La democracia en México.* México: Ediciones Era, 1965.

González Pineda, Francisco. *El mexicano: su dinámica psicosocial,* 3d. ed. México, D.F.: Editorial Pax-México, 1966.

Guzmán, Martín Luis. *La sombra del caudillo,* 2d. ed. Madrid: Espasa-Calpe, 1930.

Iturriaga, José E. *La estructura social y cultural de México.* México, D.F.: Fondo de Cultura Económica, 1951.

Kahl, Joseph. *The Measurement of Modernism: a Study of Values in Brazil and Mexico.* Austin: Published for the Institute of Latin American Studies by the University of Texas Press, 1968.

Lewis, Oscar. *The Children of Sanchez: Autobiography of a Mexican Family.* New York: Random House, 1961.

———. *Five Families: Mexican Case Studies in the Culture of Poverty.* New York: Basic Books, 1959.

———. *Life in a Mexican Village: Tepotzlán Restudied.* Urbana: University of Illinois Press, 1951.

Lieuwen, Edwin. *Arms and Politics in Latin America,* revised ed. New York: Praeger, 1961.

———. *Mexican Militarism.* Albuquerque: University of New Mexico Press, 1968.

Lozoya, Jorge Alberto. *El ejército mexicano (1911-1965).* México: El Colegio de México, 1970.

McAlister, Lyle, *et al. The Military in Latin American Sociopolitical Evolution: Four Case Studies.* Washington, D.C.: American University Center for Research in Social Systems, 1970.

Maldonado, Braulio. *Baja California,* 2d. ed. México: Costa-Amic, 1960.

Manjárrez, Froylán C. *La jornada institucional.* México, D.F.: Talleres Gráficos, 1930.

México: Cincuenta años de revolución. (4 vols.) México: Fondo de Cultura Económica, 1960, 1961, 1962.

Needler, Martin C. *Political Development in Latin America: Instability, Violence and Evolutionary Change.* New York: Random House, 1968.

Nicholson, Irene. *The X in Mexico: Growth Within Tradition.* Garden City, N.Y.: Doubleday, 1966.

Padgett, L. Vincent. *The Mexican Political System.* Boston: Houghton Mifflin, 1966.

Paz, Octavio. *The Labyrinth of Solitude.* Translated by Lysander Kemp. New York: Grove Press, 1961.

Portes Gil, Emilio. *Autobiografía de la revolución mexicana.* México: Instituto Mexicano de Cultura, 1964.

———. *La crisis política de la revolución y la próxima elección presidencial.* México, D.F.: Ediciones Botas, 1957.

———. *Quince años de política mexicana,* 2d. ed. México: Ediciones Botas, 1941.

Prewitt, Virginia. *Reportage on Mexico.* New York: E. P. Dutton, 1941.

Ramírez, Santiago. *El mexicano: psicología de sus motivaciones,* 4th ed. México, D.F.: Editorial Pax-México, 1966.

Ramos, Samuel. *Profile of Man and Culture in Mexico.* Translated by Peter G. Earle. Austin: University of Texas Press, 1962.

Rivera, Diego, and Bertram Wolfe. *Portrait of Mexico.* New York: Covici, Friede, 1937.

Romanell, Patrick. *Making of the Mexican Mind.* Lincoln: University of Nebraska Press, 1952.

Ross, Stanley, ed. *Is the Mexican Revolution Dead?* New York: Knopf, 1966.

Schmitt, Karl M. *Communism in Mexico: a Study in Political Frustration.* Austin: University of Texas Press, 1965.

Scott, Robert E. *Mexican Government in Transition.* Urbana: University of Illinois Press, 1959.

Shafer, Robert. *Mexico: Mutual Adjustment Planning.* Syracuse: Syracuse University Press, 1966.

Silva Herzog, Jesús. *El agrarismo mexicano y la reforma agraria: exposición y crítica,* 2d. ed. México, D.F.: Fondo de Cultura Económica, 1964.

———. *Breve historia de la revolución mexicana* (2 vols.), 2d. ed. México: Fondo de Cultura Económica, 1966.

Stavenhagen, Rodolfo, *et al. Neolatifundismo y explotación.* México: Editorial Nuestro Tiempo, 1968.

Tannenbaum, Frank. *Mexico: the Struggle for Peace and Bread.* New York: Knopf, 1950.

Tucker, William P. *The Mexican Government Today.* Minneapolis: University of Minnesota Press, 1957.

Turner, Frederick C. *The Dynamic of Mexican Nationalism*. Chapel Hill: University of North Carolina Press, 1968.

Ugalde, Antonio. *Power and Conflict in a Mexican Community: A Study of Political Integration*. Albuquerque: University of New Mexico Press, 1970.

Vázquez de Knauth, Josefina. *Nacionalismo y educación en México*. México, D.F.: El Colegio de México, 1970.

Vernon, Raymond. *The Dilemma of Mexico's Development: the Roles of the Private and Public Sectors*. Cambridge, Mass.: Harvard University Press, 1963.

Weyl, Nathaniel and Sylvia. *The Reconquest of Mexico: the Years of Lázaro Cárdenas*. London and New York: Oxford University Press, 1939.

Whetten, Nathan L. *Rural Mexico*. Chicago: University of Chicago Press, 1948.

Wilkie, James W. *The Mexican Revolution: Federal Expenditure and Social Change Since 1910*. Berkeley and Los Angeles: University of California Press, 1967.

———., and Edna Monzón de Wilkie. *México visto en el siglo XX: entrevistas de historia oral*. México: Instituto Mexicano de Investigaciones Económicas, 1969.

Wolf, Eric. *Sons of the Shaking Earth*. Chicago: Chicago University Press, 1959.

Womack, John Jr. *Zapata and the Mexican Revolution*. New York: Knopf, 1969.

II. DISSERTATIONS, MONOGRAPHS, UNPUBLISHED PAPERS

Alschuler, Lawrence R. "Algunas consecuencias políticas de la urbanización rápida en México," mimeographed unpublished paper, University of Hawaii, June 1969.

———. *Political Participation and Urbanization in Mexico*. Ph.D. dissertation, Northwestern University, 1967.

Balán, Jorge, *et al*. *Movilidad social, migración, y fecundidad en Monterrey metropolitano*. Monterrey: Centro de Investigaciones Económicas de la Universidad de Nuevo León, 1967.

Blough, William J. "Party Identification and Political Attitudes in Mexico," mimeographed unpublished paper, University of Houston, April 1968.

Cott, Kennett. "Trends in Mexican Migration," unpublished paper, University of New Mexico, 1968.

Dovring, Folke. *Land Reform and Productivity: the Mexican Case, Anal-*

ysis of Census Data, mimeographed paper, University of Wisconsin Land Tenure Center (LTC 63), January 1969.

Goodspeed, Stephen S. *The Role of the Chief Executive in Mexico.* Ph.D. dissertation, University of California, Berkeley, 1947.

Kaufman, Clifford. "Urbanization and Political Involvement: Limited Reflections on the Case of Mexico City." (Paper prepared for delivery at the 1968 Annual Meeting of the American Political Science Association), Washington, D.C.: American Political Science Association, 1968.

Margiotta, Franklin D. *The Mexican Military: A Case Study in Nonintervention.* M.A. thesis, Georgetown University, June 1968.

Myren, Delbert T. "Integrating the Rural Market into the National Economy of Mexico," mimeographed unpublished paper, University of Wisconsin Land Tenure Center (LTC 46), June 1968.

Padgett, Leon Vincent. *Popular Participation in the Mexican "One-Party" System.* Ph.D. dissertation, Northwestern University, 1955.

Price, John A. "The Urbanization of Mexico's Northern Border States," mimeographed unpublished paper, San Diego State College, February 1969.

Reyna, José Luis. *Algunos aspectos políticos de México.* Tesis para el título de licenciado en ciencias sociales, Universidad Nacional Autónoma de México, 1967.

Segovia, Rafael. "El PRI en la coyuntura política actual," mimeographed unpublished paper, El Colegio de México, 1968.

Tuohy, William S., and Barry Ames. *Mexican Students in Politics: Rebels Without Allies?* Social Science Foundation and Graduate School of International Affairs, University of Denver, monograph series, 1970.

III. ARTICLES, CHAPTERS OF BOOKS

Alisky, Marvin. "Budgets of State Governments in Mexico," *Public Affairs Bulletin,* vol. 5, no. 2, Bureau of Governmental Research, Arizona State University, 1966.

Ames, Barry. "Bases of Support for Mexico's Dominant Party," *American Political Science Review,* vol. 64, no. 1, March 1970.

Blanksten, George I. "Foreign Policy of Mexico" in Roy Macridis, ed., *Foreign Policy in World Politics,* 2d. ed., Englewood Cliffs, N.J.: Prentice-Hall, 1962.

Cochrane, James D. "Educational Experiences of Latin American Cabinet Members: a Three-Country Study," *Comparative Educational Review,* June 1967.

Cornelius, Wayne A., Jr. "Urbanization as an Agent in Latin American Political Instability: the Case of Mexico," *American Political Science Review,* September 1969.

Cuevas Cancino, Francisco. "The Foreign Policy of Mexico" in Joseph E. Black and Kenneth W. Thompson, *Foreign Policies in a World of Change*, New York: Harper and Row, 1963.

Fried, Robert C. "Mexico City" in William A. Robson, ed., *Great Cities of the World: Their Government, Politics, and Planning*, 3d. ed., London: Allen & Unwin, 1971.

Garza, David T. "Factionalism in the Mexican Left: The Frustration of the MLN," *Western Political Quarterly*, September 1964.

Germani, Gino. "La ciudad como mecanismo integrador," *Revista Mexicana de Sociología*, vol. 29, no. 3, July-September, 1967.

Goldrich, Daniel. "Toward a Comparative Study of Politicization" in Dwight B. Heath and Richard N. Adams, eds., *Contemporary Cultures and Societies of Latin America*, New York: Random House, 1965.

González Navarro, Moisés. "Mexico: The Lop-Sided Revolution" in Claudio Veliz, ed., *Obstacles to Change in Latin America*, London and New York: Oxford University Press, 1969.

Gullahorn, Jeanne E., and Charles P. Loomis. "A Comparison of Social Distance Attitudes in the United States and Mexico," *Studies in Comparative International Development*, vol. 2, no. 4, 1966.

Hewes, Gordon W. "Mexicans in Search of the 'Mexican': Notes on Mexican National Character Studies," *American Journal of Economics and Sociology*, January 1954.

Inkeles, Alex. "The Modernization of Man" in Myron Weiner, ed., *Modernization: the Dynamics of Growth*, New York: Basic Books, 1966.

Johnson, Kenneth F. "Ideological Correlates of Right Wing Political Alienation in Mexico," *American Political Science Review*, September 1965.

Lander, Patricia, Michael Maccoby, and Nancy Modiano. "Games and Social Character in a Mexican Village," *Psychiatry*, vol. 27, no. 2, May 1964.

Lewis, Oscar. "Mexico Since Cárdenas" in Richard N. Adams, *et al., Social Change in Latin America Today: Its Implications for United States Policy*, New York: Harper, 1960.

Maccoby, Michael. "Love and Authority: A Study of Mexican Villagers," *Atlantic*, vol. 213, no. 3, March 1964.

———. "On Mexican National Character," *The Annals*, March 1967.

Mangin, William. "Latin American Squatter Settlements: A Problem and A Solution," *Latin American Research Review*, vol. II, no. 3, summer 1967.

Morse, Richard N. "Urban Society in Contemporary Latin America," *Ventures*, vol. VII, no. 2, fall 1967.

Needleman, Carolyn and Martin. "Who Rules Mexico? A Critique of

Some Current Views of the Mexican Political Process," *Journal of Politics,* vol. 31, no. 4, November 1969.

Needler, Martin C. "Changing the Guard in Mexico," *Current History,* January 1965.

———. "Mexico as a Case Study in Political Development," *International Development Review,* vol. X, no. 1, March 1968.

———. "Mexico at the Crossroads," *Current History,* February 1971.

———. "The Political Development of Mexico," *American Political Science Review,* vol. 55, no. 2, June 1961.

Padgett, Leon Vincent. "Mexico's One-Party System: a Re-evaluation," *American Political Science Review,* vol. 51, no. 4, December 1957.

Prewitt, Virginia. "The Mexican Army Today," *Foreign Affairs,* April 1941.

Rogler, Lloyd. "Slum Neighborhoods in Latin America," *Journal of Inter-American Studies,* vol. IX, no. 4, October 1967.

Sarames, George N. "Third System in Latin America: Mexico," *Inter-American Economic Affairs,* spring 1952.

Scott, Robert E. "Budget Making in Mexico," *Inter-American Economic Affairs,* autumn 1955.

Segovia, Rafael. "El nacionalismo mexicano: los programas políticos revolucionarios (1929-1964)," *Foro Internacional,* vol. 8, no. 4, April-June 1968.

Stavenhagen, Rodolfo. "Marginalidad y participación en la reforma agraria mexicana," *Revista Latinoamericana de Sociología,* vol. 5, no. 2, July 1969.

———. "Un modelo para el estudio de las organizaciones políticas en México," *Revista Mexicana de Sociología,* vol. 29, no. 2, April-June 1967.

Taylor, Philip B., Jr. "The Mexican Elections of 1958: Affirmation of Authoritarianism?" *Western Political Quarterly,* September 1960.

Unikel Spector, Luis. "Ensayo sobre una nueva clasificación de población rural y urbana en México," *Demografía y Economía,* vol. 2, no. 1, 1968.

———. "El caso de México," *Revista de la Sociedad Interamericana de Planificación,* vol. 2, nos. 5 and 6, marzo-junio, 1968.

Williamson, Jeffrey G. "Regional Inequality and the Process of National Development: A Description of the Patterns," *Economic Development and Cultural Change,* vol. 13, no. 4, Part II, July 1965.

INDEX

INDEX

141